SEARCHING
FOR TRUTH

Other books in the Foundations of Christian Faith series
Christian Worship by Ronald P. Byars
The Trinity by Philip W. Butin
What It Means to Be Human by Michelle J. Bartel

SEARCHING FOR TRUTH

*Confessing Christ
in an Uncertain World*

Thomas W. Currie III

Foundations of Christian Faith
Published by Geneva Press in Conjunction with
the Office of Theology and Worship, Presbyterian Church (U.S.A.)

Book design by Sharon Adams
Cover design by Night & Day Design

First edition
Published by Geneva Press
Louisville, Kentucky

This book is printed on acid-free paper that meets the American National Standards Institute Z39.48 standard. ∞

PRINTED IN THE UNITED STATES OF AMERICA

01 02 03 04 05 06 07 08 09 10 — 10 9 8 7 6 5 4 3 2 1

Library of Congress Cataloging-in-Publication Data

Currie, Thomas W.
    Searching for truth : confessing Christ in an uncertain world / Thomas W. Currie III.—1st ed.
        p. cm.—(Foundations of Christian faith)
    Includes bibliographical references.
    ISBN 0-664-50139-7 (alk. paper)
      1. Truth—Religious aspects—Christianity. 2. Bible. N.T. Gospels—Criticism, interpretations, etc. I. Title. II. Series

BT50.C87 2001
230—dc21   2001023130

"Truth without love kills, but love without truth lies."
Eberhard Arnold

This book is dedicated to the two congregations I have had the privilege of pastoring: the Brenham Presbyterian Church in Brenham, Texas, and First Presbyterian Church in Kerrville, Texas. Just as no one does theology alone, so no one pastors alone. Any pastor worth his salt will tell you how much he has been pastored by the congregations he has served. This has certainly been the case with me. I want to thank these congregations who have loved me and who have taught me what it means to confess the truth that Jesus Christ, the Crucified, is Lord. I am grateful to have walked with them for a while in his service.

Contents

Series Foreword

*T*he books in the Foundations of Christian Faith series explore central elements of Christian belief. These books are intended for persons on the edge of faith as well as for those with strong Christian commitment. The writers are women and men of vital faith and keen intellect who know what it means to be an everyday Christian.

Each of the twelve books in the series focuses on a theme central to the Christian faith. The authors hope to encourage you as you grapple with the big, important issues that accompany our faith in God. Thus, Foundations of Christian Faith includes volumes on the Trinity, what it means to be human, worship and sacraments, Jesus Christ, the Bible, the Holy Spirit, the church, life as a Christian, political and social engagement, religious pluralism, creation and new creation, and dealing with suffering.

You may read one or two of the books that deal with issues you find particularly interesting, or you may wish to read them all in order to gain a deeper understanding of your faith. You may read the books by yourself or together with others. In any event, I trust that you will find a fuller awareness of the living God who is made known in Jesus Christ through the present power of the Holy Spirit. Christian faith is not about the mastery of ideas. It is about encountering the living God. It is my confident hope that this series of books will lead you more deeply into that encounter.

Charles Wiley
Office of Theology and Worship
Presbyterian Church (U.S.A.)

Acknowledgments

One of the themes of this book is that no one can be a Christian alone. The writing of this book has reminded me how dependent I am on the witness, the encouragement, the patience and even the faith of my brothers and sisters in Christ.

I want particularly to thank John Burgess who, before he left the General Assembly's Office of Theology and Worship to teach at Pittsburgh Seminary, recommended me for this assignment. I also want to thank Charles Wiley, who took John's place in that office, for his encouragement, advice, quick wit, and generous support. Both Charles and John have worked in tandem with Joe Small, the coordinator of Theology and Worship, and he too has been generous with suggestions on how to proceed. I want to thank him and, in particular, his wife, Valerie, for sharing so lavishly the food and hospitality of their home on more than one occasion.

This book is one in a series of books. It has been written in deliberate conversation with several of the other authors involved in the Foundations of Christian Faith series. I want to thank them for their sensitive reading, helpful criticism, and thoughtful suggestions. I have learned from them all. I am particularly grateful to Michelle Bartel, Ron Byars, and Kathryn Cameron for their close reading of this manuscript and their willingness to speak the truth in love to me.

Most of this book was written in Dallas, at the Bridwell Library of SMU's Perkins School of Theology. During the summer of 1999, the congregation I have the privilege of serving (First Presbyterian Church, Kerrville, Texas) generously gave me a sabbatical leave of several weeks. My sister, Liz Williams, made her home available to me in Dallas and patiently listened to some of my ideas as they were first being formulated. I want to thank her for that and for steering me toward the helpful folks at the Bridwell Library. Jorge Cruz, who was in charge of the circulation desk there, proved a great help. I also want to thank Judy Stephenson, Frances Hatch, and Candice Scott of the Logan Library at Schreiner College.

I want to thank the members of the Tuesday Morning Bible Class of my congregation for their reading of chapter 5. Margaret Syers, a member of that class and a former English teacher, has done her best to keep my grammar and syntax straight, a difficult matter given my tangled thoughts. I remain deeply grateful for her efforts and for her friendship. My colleague George Kluber has been supportive of this project from its inception and has put me on to various books and offered his own valuable insights concerning the issues raised in chapter 6. I am grateful also to Ruthie Douglass, who read much of the manuscript and offered many valuable suggestions and comments. I taught chapter 4 to an adult class at the church and I have been helped by their comments. Finally, I would like to thank my wife, Peggy, for her reading of the manuscript and for her support throughout this effort.

1

Confessing Christ as an Act of Love

As the old pickup truck waited for the light to change, I could barely read the bumper sticker that was peeling off its back panel. It proclaimed simply, "God said it, I believe it, and that settles it!"

Why, I wondered, did this exercise in public theology irritate me so? Was it because these sentiments, like so many expressed in the lingo of bumper stickers, seemed less an invitation to thoughtful discussion than to confrontation and dismissal? Was it the rapid-fire, in-your-face assertiveness that bothered me, or merely the conclusions themselves? As I ruminated on these matters, the car behind me let me know that the light had turned green and it was time to move on. Thinking about faith has a way of distracting us from the business at hand, but there are times when such distractions are worth it. Indeed, there are times when such distractions, like the "distraction" of worship itself, are the one thing that makes life as sweet as it is.

So let us distract ourselves for a moment in order to consider something out of the ordinary. Let us talk, for a moment, about God. What, if anything, is really wrong with saying, "God said it, I believe it, and that settles it!"?

Assuming for the moment that "it" refers to scripture and more particularly to the gospel of Jesus Christ, then much of what the bumper sticker says is true. "In the beginning was the Word," John tells us, "and the Word was with God, and the Word was God" (John 1:1). "Then God said, 'Let there be light'; and there was light," Genesis 1:3 reminds us. Scripture may well be the record of what Israel and the church remembered of God's mighty acts, but the heart of its message is that this story is from God. It is not a story contrived by human art or skill, but it comes from God's gracious self-giving, the Word made flesh making possible the word written and proclaimed. Just so, it is rightly called God's word. God said it. So far so good.

It is also true that we believe it. Surely, that is what God's word has ever called forth: a community of faith, which entrusts its life to that Word made flesh. The church may often seem to us a disappointing result of Jesus' ministry, but the truth is that everywhere this story has been told, a community of faith has arisen. Jesus evokes not mere interest or grudging admiration but faith, and faith, moreover, that gathers itself around his word to become a community. We believe it.

So if it is true that God said it, and if it is true that we believe it, then what is left to offend? There is that little matter of it all being settled. "God said it, I believe it, *and that settles it!*" In truth, that is where the problem begins. To come to such a conclusion is to profess that in "settling" it, there is about God's word that kind of clinching certainty that no longer requires us to bear with our neighbor or struggle with scripture's own judgments or risk living out its invitations. Instead, God's word becomes the final term in an airtight equation.

But if God in fact really said "it," and if "it" is that word about Jesus Christ, then to believe in this word is precisely not to offer this world an airtight argument, much less dismiss its doubts or fears. Rather, it is to be of good cheer in the face of such doubts and fears. Why? Because not an argument but Jesus Christ has overcome this world, and it is his unsettling presence that continues to surprise us, especially in his invitation to embrace the world he loves even with all of its silly pride and quiet despair. "In the world you face persecution. But take courage; I have conquered the world!" (John 16:33).

The remarkable thing about God's word is how unsettling it has always been. When Herod heard of the birth of the Christ child in Bethlehem, he was troubled, as was "all Jerusalem with him"

(Matt. 2:3). Indeed, he was so troubled that when the wise men did not return, he flew into a rage and slaughtered innocent children in the hopes of ridding himself of this threat. This word unsettled the disciples, taking them from their comfortable world of nets and boats to the more perilous seas of fishing for God's children. Saul was unsettled into being Paul and never got over it, marveling at the length and breadth of God's hospitality to the Gentiles in Jesus Christ. The history of Israel, from Abraham and Sarah to Joshua and Deborah, is a history of God's unsettling love, calling a husband and his wife to leave their settled existence for a land they did not know, calling a people out of the settled world of slavery to that much more complicated world of liberation and faithfulness. How settled was Jonah at the end of the day, when all of his plans had gone awry and God's forgiveness had triumphed again? Or Jeremiah, watching the exiles being taken off into captivity, his country destroyed, and deciding now was the time to hope by investing in the real estate of his homeland? Or Elijah, fleeing from Ahab and convinced that he alone was faithful out of all Israel? No, whatever else the Word of God meant for them, it meant, as it did for Jacob at the brook of Jabbok, a kind of wrestling that put their limbs out of joint, a blessing that made them limp, a truth whose invitation to love persistently undermined their efforts to "settle things."

The great temptation that the bumper sticker holds out for us is the possibility of worshiping God without the embarrassment of limping. We would prefer to read God's truth in the light of our certainties. In this we are like those two sad disciples on the road to Emmaus who thought they could dismiss the dullard who had fallen into step with them by explaining to him why, given what had happened in Jerusalem, there was really no more reason to hope. Just so are our "dead certainties" always ambushed by the grace of the risen Lord. And just so are we unsettled, invited to trust in him even more than in our clinching arguments, none of which calls us, as he does, to love the world we are so eager to dismiss.

The fact is that we lust for a truth that will not embarrass us nearly so much, a truth that would have the good sense to remain disembodied and neat, unentangled in any particular culture or history. Such a truth would possess a universal certainty that would be obvious even to unbelievers. Indeed, that would be one of its great strengths, a truth whose certainty would occupy that neutral space where all right-thinking folk could gather and give their assent without risking their good names. Such a truth would no longer even require of us faith.

Indeed, that is the oddest thing of all about the pickup truck's bumper sticker: it lacks faith. In its eagerness to have things settled, it betrays an embarrassment with a faith that can at best, only see "through a glass dimly," a faith that must ask for the illumination of the Holy Spirit. Such an embarrassment even extends to an impatience with life in a community that limps. Rather, it seeks to hurry on, to put the whole matter of its limping behind, even to move beyond faith, to that happier realm of our own decisions, where only our choosing finally matters.

Perhaps you think I have been too hard on this poor old bumper sticker and have, in any case, spent far too much time picking at its innards. Perhaps I have, though as I hope will become clear, I also have some admiration for its willingness to say what it believes. But it does seem to me that in its desire for a kind of unquestionable certitude, the bumper sticker is worshiping at one of the most compelling idols of modern culture. That idol can be identified with what Lesslie Newbigin calls "the certitude of self," a conviction that he contrasts with scripture's description of the "faithfulness of God."[1] Certitude of self begins with myself as the most certain thing of all, and claims that all of reality is to be read in light of that starting point. The truth is simply too important a thing to be left in God's hands. Here we must begin with ourselves, guaranteeing a notion of truth that can be universally determined without reference to Israel's particular history or God's singular self-giving in Jesus Christ. Here, frankly, God is not to be trusted. As scripture itself reminds us, God is not under our control, which is why, given our certitude of self, we find it so much easier to doubt God's existence than to follow his commandments.

But I do not want to leave my friend in the pickup truck. It would be a mistake to conclude that certitude of self is only his problem. The desire to speak of God in terms of what we take to be more certain than God—that is, ourselves and our own experience—that desire is as American as apple pie. Indeed, Harold Bloom has called the impulse to begin with ourselves and our own experience, "the American religion."[2] It is precisely what allows us to pretend that we are a nation of 280 million "jealous gods," each requiring an elaborate legal apparatus to keep one from stepping on the toe of the other. Our songs are always of "myself." That is why it is so difficult for us to talk to one another. Who can really know what it is like to be me? Or you? Indeed, in some extreme forms, this certitude of self can almost convince me that you are barely there at all, or at best have only a kind of marginal existence. This truth is unrelated to others. It begins and ends with "me." And as our culture has fragmented into smaller and smaller communities of self, so has it become an increasingly lonely place, the more lonely as we move more and more to the center of our own little worlds.

That is why it would be a mistake to dismiss that old pickup truck with its bumper sticker as somehow beneath our contempt, or to pretend that the assertion of its claims is what is wrong with our understanding of the faith. In truth, I admire that old truck and suspect that its driver has a good deal to say to us. He, after all, is willing to risk stating his convictions in the hurly-burly of public discourse and life. He, after all, is confident that there is someone besides himself in the world. He, after all, believes in that God who speaks and who calls forth from us a response of faith. He has not yet learned to be so suspicious of the truth as to keep his faith private, or worse, to give up on the whole notion of the truth while settling instead for what is merely "truth for me." If anything, the driver of this pickup truck believes that what is true for him is probably true for the rest of us, which is why he has a bumper sticker for us to read in the first place.

If he appears angry or dismissive to us, it may well be because we resent having our privacy invaded by his claims. Being compelled to answer for our faith is not something we are used to doing. We would rather keep our options open. We rather like hearing about the unsettling nature of the gospel because it implies, we think, that matters will never be settled, that we can keep our options open indefinitely. The bumper sticker's theology, however inadequate it might be, still has not stooped to the level of concluding that there is no truth worth proclaiming, no gospel worth sharing, no life worth giving away. It still has something to say to the world. And its own words, however abrasive and even rude we might find them, describe a world that is not quite as lonely as ours sometimes seems, nor quite as hopeless.

We are caught then between a kind of bumper sticker defiance whose faith is only too ready to dismiss the world and a kind of nonjudgmental privacy that wishes only to be left alone and has given up any claim to a truth larger than its own happiness. Neither of these options is satisfactory and both are strategies we have developed to keep from having to deal with the radical claims of Jesus Christ in our world. Throwing "the truth" as if it were a rock at a culture that rightly suspects we do not possess the truth, deeply betrays both the truth of Jesus Christ and the dignity of those whom he calls us to love. There is something about the gospel that does not make a good rock, that resists being thrown at someone. Rather, this gospel, while universal in its claims, is, nevertheless, utterly giftlike in its proclamation, evoking within those who receive its grace (*charis*), thanksgiving (*eucharis*).

Giving up on the truthfulness of the gift, however, is perhaps even more contemptuous in its ingratitude. Such a retreat into "modesty" can only justify itself by offering to "save" the truth of the gospel by narrowing its scope, by keeping it private, safe, harmless, and in the end, domesticating it to our own tender mercies. How strong a temptation this is can be seen in our own reluctance to profess the gospel as true. Therapeutic, yes; instructive, no doubt; good for us, certainly. But true? We are afraid to venture such an affirmation because we think it might well give offense, or worse, because we ourselves are such poor arguments for its truth. So we content ourselves with the gospel being "true for me," and our retreat from anything more daring results, as Emily Dickinson knew very well, in making our behavior small.[3]

How then can we get past this dilemma? How can we speak the truth as truth, yet speak it in love? How can we confess Jesus Christ without that confession being merely a rock we throw at a culture we are only too ready to dismiss, or worse, without reducing its gospel truth to something we find manageable and, finally, harmless? These are the questions that this book will attempt to answer.

Telling the Truth as an Act of Love

How does God tell the truth? That may seem to be a silly question, but it is not. We think of God as being in the truth business, rather like we think of God as being in the forgiveness business. But in fact, it is not obvious that God should tell the truth at all. Many of the gods of Greek and Roman mythology were celebrated for their cunning and deceptiveness, not for telling the truth. The witches in *Macbeth*, like the Furies in ancient mythology, are godlike in their knowledge of the future, but they are hardly trustworthy. Rather, "they tell us truths," and "win us with honest trifles," only "to betray us in deepest consequence."[4]

The God of Israel, on the other hand, is celebrated because "the promise of the LORD proves true" (Ps. 18:30). "The Lord is faithful in all his words, and gracious in all his deeds" (Ps. 145:13). This God's love is "steadfast" and "endures forever" (Ps. 107:1). "Know therefore that the LORD your God is God," Moses tells the children of Israel before they enter the Promised Land, "the faithful God who maintains covenant loyalty with those who love him" (Deut. 7:9). This God desires "truth in the inward being," and knows what is in our "secret heart" (Ps. 51:6).

In all of this, Israel's God is celebrated not so much for merely telling the truth as for living the truth, keeping faith, fulfilling the terms of the promise: "so shall my word be that goes out from my mouth; it shall not return to me empty, but it shall accomplish that which I purpose, and succeed in the thing for which I sent it" (Isa. 55:11). In this act of promise and fulfillment, God establishes his life of faithfulness with Israel: "I will be your God and you will be my people," a promise Israel understands to be a repetition of God's original covenant with Abraham. That promise Israel knows to be a blessing, not just because it tells of Israel being chosen but even more because it narrates Yahweh's faithful and "steadfast love."

And that is why this Old Testament notion of truth is so remarkable. Rather than being a virtue that God possesses or a mental capacity able to specify what is the case, God's truth is an act of loving, of keeping faith with those whom he has called, of keeping faith with them even when there is no good reason to do so. That is God's character, the way this God tells the truth, by living it out of his own life. Such a truth is less a propositional statement than it is a relationship of love, a demonstration of the freedom in which God is able to turn toward "the other" and live faithfully in relation to that other. Telling the truth in terms of this kind of steadfast love is, Christians believe, descriptive of a personally related God, indeed, descriptive of the very life of God the Father, Son, and Holy Spirit.

It is hard for us to think about the truth in terms of such love, but that is only because we have gotten used to thinking of it in less personal ways. The truth for us is something more neutral, and often has very little to do with love. It has, rather, to do with "facts," or perhaps more often with what a clever contemporary philosopher has defined as being, namely, "whatever my colleagues will let me get away with."[5] To be sure, the modern world has a great deal invested in keeping the truth neutral, for by doing so we enable ourselves to think we are in control of it and can manage it as an instrument for our own purposes and in the best interest of others. Part of the price of this illusion, however, has been that the truth has become suspect for us; even worse, our notion of love has been emptied of much of its content. By separating love from truth, we have thought it possible to enjoy relationships that are not so costly, and deal with truths that are not so entangling. It is disconcerting, therefore, to find the truth of Israel's God so persistently well defined in terms of "steadfast love." Such a definition suggests the disturbing possibility that the way this God tells the truth, far from being neutral, is deeply personal. It threatens to take us beyond our depths and involve us in a relationship of love we cannot escape, in a life that challenges our most settled definitions.

What would such a telling of the truth look like? The Gospel of John describes it in this way: "For God so loved the world that he gave his only Son, so that everyone who believes in him may not perish but may have eternal life. Indeed, God did not send the Son into the world to condemn the world, but in order that the world might be saved through him" (John 3:16–17).

The Christian faith has always affirmed that Jesus Christ is the basic way God tells the truth. For in him, "the Word became flesh and lived among us, . . . full of grace and truth" (John 1:14). This truth is intensely personal. "I am the way, and the truth, and the life," Jesus tells his disciples. "No one comes to the Father except through me"(John 14:6). Indeed, so personal is this truth that some of its best teachers are Jesus' opponents. Herod rightly recognizes what is at stake in the birth of this child. His kingdom—indeed, every human kingdom—is threatened by the claims of this child. The demons unfailingly recognize what kind of truth they are up against in Jesus, even confessing him "Son of the Most High God" (Mark 5:7) long before the disciples do. The rich young man understands Jesus only too well in turning sorrowfully away (Matt. 19:22). And the Pharisees are utterly right to believe that if Jesus embodies God's truth, their world of carefully calibrated truths and laws is doomed. They comprehend exactly the scope of Jesus' message, which is why it finally becomes urgent for them and others to have Jesus discredited and even killed.

Only the disciples seem to press for a more neutral understanding of the truth. Having confessed Jesus as the Messiah, the Son of God, and having received Jesus' blessing, Peter is offended when Jesus describes how the truth of God will get itself told through suffering and death. "God forbid, Lord," Peter replies. The truth need not be taken so personally. "This shall not happen to you." And Jesus' words in reply are sharper than anything he ever says to the Pharisees: "Get behind me, Satan! You are a stumbling block to me; for you are setting your mind not on divine things but on human things" (Matt. 16:23).

Time and time again the disciples miss the radical nature of God's telling the truth as an act of love. But in all four Gospels, such steadfast love leads inexorably to the cross, to the place where God's truth becomes visible in an almost unbearably personal way, a way of telling the truth from which we almost want to shield our eyes. This truth involves dying. There's no getting around that. Yet such a death becomes for us strangely fruitful, a "Good Friday," a day on which we see the crucial way God speaks the truth in love and redeems the world through the death of his own Son. "Unless a grain of wheat falls into the earth and dies, it remains just a single grain; but if it dies, it bears much fruit" (John 12:24). Such a telling of the truth is the way God loves this world, the way Jesus draws all to himself (John 12:32). It is the way of the cross, the way of a suffering love that unashamedly identifies itself with sinners and is content, at the end, even to die with them in that strange community of the Crucified. There the circle of God's love in being Father, Son, and Holy Spirit extends to sinners and in Jesus Christ carries us to the very heart of God's own life. It is this act of love, we believe, that tells us the truth, and in light of which we risk understanding ourselves and our world. Whatever else we might think of a broken and sinful world, the way of the cross refuses to let us abdicate our way into something smaller, even when we think it would be more modest and less embarrassing. No, God's way of telling the truth seeks something bigger than our comfortably private hells; it seeks nothing less than "the freedom of the glory of the children of God" (Rom. 8:21). It is this truth that is revealed in all of its stunning glory on Easter Sunday, a truth that not even death could settle.

But if the cross is the way God tells the truth, the way steadfast love unsettles our certainties in bringing us within the circle of God's love, how then will we ever be able to tell such a truth? Are we given some special capacity for suffering or some deeper vision that other folks do not have? Clearly not. All we are given as Christians to begin on this journey is our baptism. To be sure, that may seem a pitifully small gift. But just so, it reminds us that the freedom to love is not a human possibility. It is not something we can manufacture by trying really hard. Here, too, we stumble. In fact, our baptism is a reminder that we belong to a community that limps and gropes its way along, seeking to follow Jesus Christ. Yet in such limping and groping, we are reminded that even here we are blessed, blessed by a truth we have not invented but have received from Christ himself. Baptism makes us like children again, learning to walk, often stumbling and falling but being drawn more deeply into Christ's fellowship, more deeply into the truth of his life. The apostle Paul puts it this way: "Do you not know that all of us who have been baptized into Christ Jesus were baptized into his death? Therefore we have been buried with him by baptism into death, so that, just as Christ was raised from the dead by the glory of the Father, so we too might walk in newness of life" (Rom. 6:3–4).

Paul's words remind us that the "newness of life" in whose truth we seek to walk has come to us as a gift of the cross. It is not something we have found and now possess so much as it has found us and drawn us into the life of God's triune love. Our problem, then, is not so much to figure out how to explain this truth as it is how to learn to walk in its newness. The temptation is always to forget that our baptism means a dying and a rising. We find it easy to think that our stumbling about is only that, a sad and inadequate way of propelling ourselves forward, not a training for a life of dancing within this circle of God's love. In truth, we grow ashamed of our awkwardness, convinced that newness of life is a farce or a feeling that can only be sustained in an environment sheltered from the harsh realities of the world. Both temptations reject the hard baptismal truth that we belong "body and soul, in life and in death— not to [ourselves] but to [our] faithful Savior, Jesus Christ."[6] Yet both temptations are powerful because their lies seem so plausible. The world in which we live often does not look like it belongs to Jesus Christ. More to the point, neither do we.

Perhaps, then, we would be both more honest and courageous simply to admit our failures and move on. Or perhaps we should be more modest about our own baptism, confining its truth to the highly ritualized world of ceremony and the cuteness of children. In any case, such temptations ask hard questions of the faith, and there is no way of proceeding except through their fires.

The Temptation to Dismiss Our Faith

In Fyodor Dostoyevsky's novel *The Brothers Karamazov*, an old priest named Father Zossima defines hell as a suffering that is unable to love. Two of the brothers, Ivan and Alyosha, struggle with what it means to love. Ivan, the intellectual and radical student, eventually despairs of loving this world because he is convinced it is a place of misery, a place where God has botched up the work of creation. The truth is, the psalmists were wrong: God is not worthy of our thanks or praise. "Newness of life" is at best a farce, at worst a lie. Ivan keeps a list of cruelties that human beings do to each other: babies bayoneted during an ethnic cleansing, children hunted down by dogs, a little girl abused by her parents. And then he turns and asks his brother, Alyosha, a novice monk:

> Can you understand why a little creature, who can't even understand what's done to her, should beat her little aching heart with her tiny fist in the dark and the cold, and weep her meek unresentful tears to dear, kind God to protect her? Do you understand that, Alyosha, you pious and humble novice? Do you understand why this infamy must be and is permitted? Without it, I am told, man could not have existed on earth, for he could not have known good and evil. Why should he know that diabolical good and evil when it costs so much? . . .
>
> And if the sufferings of children go to swell the sum of sufferings which was necessary to pay for truth, then I protest that the truth is not worth such a price. . . . Is there in the whole world a person who would have the right to forgive and could forgive? I don't want harmony. From love for humanity I don't want it. . . . Besides, too high a price is asked for harmony; it's beyond our means to pay so much. And so I give back my entrance ticket, and if I am an honest man I give it back as soon as possible. . . . It's not God that I don't accept, Alyosha, only I most respectfully return the ticket to Him.[7]

"That's rebellion," Alyosha replies, but Ivan is content to be a rebel who dissents from such a God. Later in the novel he goes further, concluding that all morality is a sham and that "without God, anything is permissible." His words eventually result in his father's murder and in the suicide of a half brother who, before he dies, taunts Ivan with his own philosophy.

Much of what Ivan observes about the world is true. It is full of injustice and not only that—it is full of injustice that will never be set right in this life, never be brought into "Euclidean balance." Ivan asks some hard questions of those who want to affirm the baptismal truth that we belong to One who numbers even the hairs of our head and who will one day wipe away every tear from our eyes. It is no good to say that Ivan has despaired of the faith. That he cheerfully admits. The question is whether the "harmony" of which Ivan despairs corresponds to the faith of Israel and the church.

Ivan's dilemma is not just that of some tormented soul in a Russian novel. It is the dilemma of any person who has ever seen unanswerable pain or irredeemable injustice. In some ways, Ivan is a very admirable figure. He does not seek to paper over the cruelties of the world, wrapping them in some sort of sentimental religion that comforts the believer even if it does no good for others. Moreover, Ivan at least knows enough about the faith to know that in its deepest sense it is a story about things being put right, about God's justice being done on earth as in heaven. But in rejecting the faith that has told him God loves this world, Ivan seeks a world that would be much more deserving of that love, that would, in some sense, justify God's love. What angers Ivan is not just that the world is a cruel place, but that it might be a place God loves. What he fears is that forgiveness itself is unjust, that grace throws things out of balance. By "returning his ticket," he hopes to settle things, to exempt himself from this sorry mess. That would, in any case, be easier than living by faith in the face of such injustice. He can no longer love this world. He no longer has the faith to do so. Indeed, that is the hell he has entered: the suffering of being unable to love.

We would not do well to explain to Ivan that things are not as bad as he thinks, that there are also many good things happening in the world, that if he just would accentuate the positive, things would look better than they do. Ivan is not in need of an airtight argument. He already has one of those. What Ivan needs is a more embodied truth, an incarnate word, the gift of a love that is not offended by suffering but rather embraces it. Ivan, like all of us, is in need of the cross. Apart from such a gift, Dostoyevsky suggests, the Ivans of this world, who love justice but despise the embarrassing humiliation of grace, will never be able to receive the gift of their own lives. Indeed, the "justice" they seek will be a graceless thing, a hell of their own invention worse than the one they describe. Ivan's mistake is that he thinks he can live out of himself and not out of the death of Christ. Self-invention has always been the enemy of baptism. But baptism is the way we receive the gift of our life in Christ, being drowned in his death and being raised to receive the astonishing gift of his quite non-Euclidean grace.

At the end of his long tale of woe, Ivan waits for Alyosha to respond and all that Alyosha can do for him is to kiss him, to kiss him as a brother who loves him. Ivan laughs at such plagiarism of Jesus' forgiveness, but just so is he reminded of the one to whom he belongs.

Alyosha's "answer" may not seem like much of an answer to those who are tempted in the face of the world's suffering to dismiss the faith in favor of some "certitude of self." But in the end, Alyosha's answer is an eloquent speaking of the truth in love. His is a happy kiss that confesses that the cross is the only truth that can redeem a broken world and save us from the despair that ensues when the world refuses to conform to our sense of justice. In a strange sort of way, such a kiss corresponds to baptism itself, pointing to a dying and rising that rejoices in God's love for this world.

The Temptation to Dismiss the World

Ivan, however, is not the only one to struggle in the novel. His brother, Alyosha, is also tempted, though in a different way. Alyosha is not tempted to dismiss his faith so much as he is tempted to dismiss the world. He would like to trim the gospel down to the size of the monastery where he is most comfortable, to keep the truth of Jesus Christ as merely a "truth for me."

His crisis is precipitated by the death of his mentor, Father Zossima, a man so holy that Alyosha fully expects him to die with a body undecayed, impervious to the corruption that afflicts common, garden-variety sinners. When this does not happen, Alyosha is thrown into a crisis of faith and seeks to escape the harsh realities of life (and death) by retreating into the more sheltered world of the monastery itself. Returning to the monastery late at night, Alyosha hears a monk reading the gospel lesson over the coffin of the dead elder. The passage is from the Gospel of John, concerning the wedding at Cana in Galilee. Alyosha listens:

> Ah, yes, I was missing that. . . . I love that passage—it's Cana of Galilee, the first miracle. . . . Ah, that sweet miracle! It was not men's grief, but their joy Christ visited. He worked his first miracle to help men's gladness. . . . His heart was open even to the simple, artless, merry-making of some obscure and unlearned people, who had warmly bidden him to their poor wedding.[8]

Praying and almost dreaming, Alyosha thinks he sees his beloved mentor, the dead Father Zossima, coming to him as one of the guests at the wedding at Cana. He invites Alyosha to look at Jesus Christ: "Do not fear him. He is terrible in his greatness, awful in his sublimity, but infinitely merciful. He has made himself like unto us from love and rejoices with us. He is changing the water into wine that the gladness of the guests may not be cut short."[9]

Alyosha awakes from his dream, but he knows he has been granted a vision of the kingdom. And he knows now that his life will not be spent in the monastery but in the world, the world of poor and often miserable people who hunger for love and whose joys are occasions of grace.

Aloysha's faith has led him not away from the world, not into a truth that will only be a "truth for him," but into the world of suffering and doubt, a world he knows to be embraced by the truth of Jesus Christ. This world may well be fully as miserable as Ivan thinks it is, but Alyosha knows a deeper truth, namely, that it is also the scene of God's mysterious grace. His faith, rather than retreating into some sheltered privacy that keeps Ivan's harsh questions at bay, turns and actively confronts them. He kisses the earth, embracing its anger and hurt, confident that in Jesus Christ it is the world in all of its joys and sorrows that God loves and redeems. So does love learn to speak the truth. And so does faith, far from narrowing our field of vision, serve to deepen it, enabling us to see the glory of God in the earthiest of realities.

Loving the World Enough to Stand within It

We are tempted then in two ways: either to think we possess the truth and can throw it at the world, or to trim this truth and make it less offensive to the world. Both temptations seek to avoid having to struggle with him who is the way, the truth, and the life. Both temptations seek to tell the truth in some safer way, in a way that does not involve limping. Yet limping is what happens to God's people when they wrestle with the truth of Jesus Christ. Indeed, it is the characteristic way we learn to speak the truth in love, the way our baptism drowns our illusions of self-sufficiency and raises us to live by grace. Such limping gives the lie to the notion that the truth is in our possession to do with as we please, just as it also subverts our clever schemes for rendering the truth harmless. When Jesus tells his disciples that he is the way, the truth, and the life, he immediately promises them the gift of the Holy Spirit, "the Spirit of truth" (John 14:17) who will "teach you everything" (John 14:26). It is this Spirit of Jesus Christ who enables us to do the impossible: to love the world enough to stand within it and speak his truth. We might well prefer to throw rocks, or worse, say nothing at all. But it is our task and our gift as Christians that we are called to speak the truth. How we do that in a world full of competing claims and clashing truths is the subject of the next chapter. But here it is sufficient to note that such a task is the gift that ever confronts those who follow Jesus Christ.

2

Loving Our Enemies:
Faith's Difficult Questions

*D*isagreement can be painful. It is especially painful when it occurs among those whom we love or over matters that we regard as important. Regulating disagreement, even helping folks to agree to disagree, is a rare gift and requires not only the virtues of patience and imagination but also a certain dogged determination not to give up when the way grows hard. Above all, it requires a commitment to listen to the painful questions persons put to each other, even bearing with them for a while and not forcing an agreement by smothering such questions under a sentimental cloud of "love," or dismissing them as unimportant or trivial. "Blessed are the peacemakers" is a beatitude not only for those negotiating peace around a green baize table but also for spouses struggling to redeem a troubled and embittered marriage or parents seeking to reconcile fractious and weary children.

When one looks at the world today, whether in the Balkans or Northern Ireland, whether in India or Pakistan, whether in Israel or its Arab neighbors, it is hard to avoid the conclusion that some of the most bitter and longstanding disagreements are between religious claims. As children of the Enlightenment, we have been well schooled on the brutal atrocities of the "wars of religion," of the Spanish Inquisition, of the crusading mentality. And our legacy of liberal democratic institutions has assured us that it was through a kind of imposition of "toleration" on religion that religion was saved from its worst impulses and absolutist demands.[1] By making society more plural, that is, by moving away from an absolutist fusion of religion and government, it was hoped that not every political question would become an ultimate one and not every ultimate question would require a political solution. Such a plural set of options offered the possibility of a more peaceful society, but also a richer and fuller society, a society in which all manner of religious convictions could be practiced in the space left vacant by governmental authority and religious establishment. This notion of pluralism, of a "mixed" society, incorporates, however modestly, a vision of what is good, a sense that life is enriched by traditions that locate and nourish our identities and teach us to listen and to act responsibly. We are right to think of a pluralistic society as a free society. The twentieth century has certainly seen enough of the opposite, of totalitarian societies, for example, in which there is only one answer for all questions.

But sometimes "pluralism" can simply be another name for that kind of smothering "love" that refuses to let questions be asked. The "toleration" that was won in England in 1688, for example, was won at the expense of not tolerating atheists and Catholics, that is, by dismissing anyone whose faith commitments (or lack thereof) might lead them to challenge the terms of such "toleration." A pluralism that tolerates all those except those who reject its terms can be a stifling thing indeed, as we have seen in our own day when religious claims have ventured into the public arena. One thinks of the debates about abortion or school prayer or, if one has a longer memory, of the civil rights movement in the South.

From the time of John Locke to the present, the pluralistic settlement that divided the world of the state from that of religion has held that freedom of religion will be granted so long as such freedom remains private and does not transgress on the state's prerogatives. When it does, then religion must defer to the state. George Will has put the matter neatly: "Religion is to be perfectly free as long as it is perfectly private . . . private and subordinate."[2]

But clearly this freedom of religion is bought with a price, namely, its acceptance of a private and a public sphere and its agreement to remain confined to the latter. Jody Fields, a respondent to a recent survey, speaks for many when she says, "If you are a Hindu, and you grew up being a Hindu, keep it to yourself. Don't impose your religion, and don't make me feel bad because I do this and you do this."[3]

Yet the one thing that devout people of any faith have never been able to do is to keep their beliefs to themselves. Whether they build a mosque or observe Sabbath rituals or protest against persecution, people of faith do not leave their faith behind when they enter the public arena. Jefferson's famous "wall" separating church and state seems to be an astonishingly permeable one. Still, if living in a pluralistic society means that one must keep one's beliefs private, then the pluralism that once held such promise for human freedom and religious expression must now appear somewhat suspect. Strangely, a settlement that originated in the hope of increasing freedom of expression in matters religious has resulted in a fear of open expression of just those convictions. As Jean Bethke Elshtain has noted:

> The general view goes like this: If I am quiet about what I believe and everybody else is quiet about what he or she believes, then nobody interferes with the rights of anybody else. But that is precisely what real believers—whether believers in Martin Luther King, Jr.'s "beloved community," or in fighting economic inequality on grounds of justice, or in opposing the current abortion regime or capital punishment—cannot do: keep quiet. To tell religious believers that they must keep quiet because to speak out would by definition be to interfere with my rights is a prescription for intolerance. It is, in effect, to tell folks they cannot really believe what they believe or be who they are.[4]

If the only way that such a pluralism can mediate disagreement, or provide space for the other, is by silencing the other, then such a pluralism has not done a very good job in helping us to live amidst our otherness. Indeed, it has done so only by trivializing that otherness, complicitly silencing its convictions and questions, and inviting us not to take such matters seriously.

A more robust pluralism, what Lesslie Newbigin has called a "committed pluralism,"[5] would not silence the other by reserving such concerns for the private realm but would challenge the whole notion of there being a public and a private realm in the first place. To engage the other without trivializing his or her questions depends on what we think about the other, indeed, what we think the nature of human life is all about. Is the other merely a political problem, a potential convert, a threat that must be removed? Is the other here by accident? Or perhaps put here for my use? How I treat the other and what I am able to hear from the other will depend on what story is narrating my story. If that story is the so-called public one, then I can only treat the other as a political problem. If that story is merely a religious one and therefore a subjective and private one, then I can only treat the other as a spiritual problem, or worse, not treat the problem at all since my truth is only "true for me." Only if I believe that there is One who has entangled my life with the other in some mysterious humanity that transcends public and private spheres am I forced to hear what the other has to say to me from the depths of his or her own convictions.

Such a robust pluralism would be difficult. It would be difficult not just because it would require that we listen to points of view with which we disagree, or take seriously ideas we find repugnant, but because it would require of us faith in Jesus Christ. That is to say, it would require a miracle. Unlike a pluralism that refrains from making any judgment about what the purpose of human life might be but bids us simply be civil in our self-chosen conversations, this vision of human life would be rooted in what God has done in the cross of Jesus Christ. Life in community, we affirm, is made possible by that act. In Jesus Christ we see the purpose of human life; that is, in him we see that we are creatures who are made for life with each other. Otherness does not threaten the God who, as Father, Son, and Holy Spirit, includes such in the Trinitarian life of his own being. In Christ, then, is where our life together begins. For this reason we are constrained to listen to the cries and questions of the other, even the stranger, even our enemies, for they are folk for whom Christ also died, and though we did not choose them, he has not chosen us without them.

What might such an encounter look like, an encounter where the question of the stranger cannot be dismissed as some private matter precisely because faith in Jesus Christ will not let us do so?

What happens when our faith compels us to hear painful questions we would only be too glad to keep in some "spiritual sphere?"

Ralph Wood tells of growing up as a Baptist in East Texas and having the gospel of Jesus Christ mediated to him through a black woman named Zuma Allen. His story is about both the truth and the strangeness of the gospel: the mysterious plurality of instruments God chooses to voice that word to us, and the uncompromising truthfulness which that Word made flesh calls us to hear.

Zuma Allen was our black maid. My family was far from wealthy but, like nearly all other white families, we had a black maid. Perhaps because black maids were paid so poorly, even schoolteacher parents like mine could afford one. I can still see this woman's long black fingers—not really black underneath but nearly pink like mine—smoothing down the collars and cuffs of my father's starched white shirts as she ironed them.

But one summer day—it must have been the summer of 1946 or 1947—I spoke a word in Zuma Allen's presence that had a devastating effect on me. No sooner had I uttered that word and seen Zuma's wounded look than I knew I had done something absolutely dreadful. I crawled under the bed and hid myself there, it seemed, for hours. I did not want to come out from that dark hole. I did not want her ever to see me again, so horribly ashamed was I for the thing I had said. I knew, in a child-like way, that I had crossed a barrier that should never have been crossed. I had demeaned and diminished another human being unforgivably.

Yet the word I had let slip was not an unusual word. It was a word that I had heard my parents use, that my friends and I frequently used, that all white people and even some black people used. It was the word that formed the basis for our segregated society. It was the word that helped "keep Negroes in their place." . . . You know the word I'm talking about. I don't need to repeat it.

Why, then, did my use of these two syllables in the presence of an illiterate black maid have such a horrifying effect on me? I assure you that it was not because I was a good little boy with an innocent soul. Like everybody else, I was already an accomplished sinner at age 4 or 5. I was devastated that summer day in 1946 or 1947 because I had first heard another word spoken to me in Sunday School and proclaimed to me in church. Perhaps, alas, I need to tell you what this other two syllable word was. It was the word "Jesus." I had read this word in the Bible and I had sung it in a Baptist group that only the bald and the gray will recognize: We were called the Sunbeams and we were taught to sing, "Jesus loves the little children, all the children of the world. Red and yellow, black and white, they are precious in his sight. Jesus loves the little children of the world."

The people who had taught me this other word did not intend for it to have such a life-reversing impact. It was supposed to be a safe word, a nice word, a sweet word. . . . Yet this was the one word that my well-intentioned preachers and teachers could not control. This word could not be tamed and house-broken because it is no ordinary word: It is the Word made flesh. Already, as a first-grader, therefore, I had been shaped without knowing it by this word, "Jesus." It had set me upon a path that would lead to a place where I did not intend to go. It was the Word that would not let me speak as I was naturally inclined to speak. It would not let me violate another human being who had been made in God's image and redeemed by God's Son, without feeling the horror of God's wrath. Thus did I hear the voice of God in the injured eyes of a black maid named Zuma Allen.[6]

There is something about the gospel that does not get itself heard until it is heard in the form of the neighbor or the stranger or the one who is, in any case, over against me and different from me. Gentiles have to confess, perhaps reluctantly, that "salvation is from the Jews" (John 4:22) and that their own salvation (as Paul thinks) has come only "to make Israel jealous" (Rom. 11:11), that is, only to occasion Israel's own confession of Jesus Christ. Thus, strangely, Jew and Gentile have to receive the gospel from each other. Scripture is full of examples where no small part of the gospel's offense stems from the embarrassing way it is mediated through the "wrong" people. One thinks of Naaman's contempt for Elisha's directive to wash in the Jordan, or of Peter's astonishment that God not only troubles his sleep with visions of a nonkosher kitchen but also speaks in dreams to Cornelius, a Roman soldier. Perhaps most astonishing of all is Paul himself, the "Hebrew of Hebrews," who, having been knocked off his horse, discovers that his mission in life is to be, of all things, an apostle to the Gentiles. It is not offensive enough that we should have to receive a gospel that invites us to love our enemies; we even have to receive the gospel from them! "Welcome one another," Paul tells a church of Jews and Gentiles, "as Christ has welcomed you" (Rom. 15:7).

Here is the real source of the Christian commitment to a pluralistic community: not in some indifferent neutrality in which all claims are accepted as equally true or false, but in the knotty yet unavoidable truth of the Word made flesh in the life, death, and resurrection of Jesus Christ. It is this truth that we cannot finesse. It is this truth that discovers among "red and yellow, black and white" folk a community of sinners for whom Christ died, sinners who are "precious in his sight." It is this truth that insists that Jesus' gift of himself to us comes only in the company of those, and often from the hands of those, whom we have not chosen but whom we are invited to receive as a gift.

Indeed, what is most remarkable about this story of receiving the gospel from a stranger is Wood's recognition that what enabled him to recognize the dreadful nature of his own offense was his being shaped already by the name of Jesus. The people who taught that name to him had no idea how subversive it was of the culture's own idolatries. They thought it a safe word, even a sweet word. Yet just so did they nurture him in the one truth that would enable him really to hear the voice of the stranger. And just so they became for that little "Sunbeam" the church of Jesus Christ.

Wood eventually left his little East Texas town and went off to college in a not much larger community. There he encountered an English professor who set him on his vocational course in life.

This Christian teacher left his deep mark on me because he was not afraid to face the toughest opponents of the gospel. Precisely in order to test the strength of his own Christianity, Paul Barrus [the teacher's name] had written his doctoral dissertation on Ralph Waldo Emerson, the great pagan saint of American literature. Only if the gospel could meet and match Emerson's paganism was it worthy of intelligent assent. . . . And so Paul Barrus taught us to have great reverence for the honest doubters of traditional Christianity. He totally immersed us Baptists in Emerson and Thoreau and Whitman, in Melville and Hawthorne and Twain. This deeply Christian teacher thus made me hear the gospel in a startlingly new way with his insistence that an unintelligent faith is a contradiction in terms. An unthink-

ing Christian, he showed us, is an affront to the God whose Son
is the Truth incarnate. This God doesn't require of us to have
brains in order to be saved, but he surely requires us to use all
the brains we've got, precisely because they're the brains he's
given us.

Yet there was a rattle in this splendid teacher's voice that I
was taught not to like. For it turns out that Paul Barrus was not
a Baptist, nor a Methodist, nor a member of the Church of Christ
or the Assemblies of God—the only four churches in my provin-
cial little East Texas town. He wasn't even a Presbyterian or a
Lutheran or Episcopalian—whoever *they* were. He wasn't even
a Protestant. God forbid, he was a Roman Catholic. Just as I had
been taught that blacks are natively inferior, so had I learned that
Catholics are not even Christians. Before I went to college, I had
only met one set of Catholics, a family who had already proved
how strange and subhuman they were by having a daughter who
was a nun. Yet here as a freshman I was confronted with the
deepest and most Christian voice I had ever heard, and it was
a Roman Catholic voice. . . . Against my will and utterly to my
surprise, this Catholic teacher released my little Baptist butterfly
from its confining cage. He turned me into an ecumenical Christian, . . . teaching not the Baptist faith narrowly construed, but
the Christian faith in its widest and deepest expressions—
Catholic and Orthodox and Protestant.[7]

Wood concludes his narrative with perhaps the oddest turn of all
in a pilgrimage of many turns. He tells of being admitted to the
University of Chicago and eventually receiving his Ph.D. there, of
leaving his East Texas Baptist provincialism behind and taking up
a teaching post at a university where he "hoped to turn my naïve
Christian students into fellow sophisticates like me." On the way
to the heavenly city of enlightened philosophy, Wood was waylaid
by the most unwanted stranger of all, a Baptist preacher named
Warren Carr.

I tried to ignore and avoid him in every way I could. He represented the constricting past whose shackles I had already
slipped. But like Jacob wrestling with the angel at the River Jabbok, this preacher would not let me go until I had blessed him.
It turned out that he too had read a lot of books, indeed that he
had written a couple. . . . Yet it was not Warren Carr's sharp mind
and wild wit that drew me to him. It was his voice. He spoke with

authority that I had never heard at the University of Chicago. It was a deliberate and careful voice, neither quick-paced nor especially eloquent. It was a voice that . . . had known deep personal suffering. It was the voice of a courageous Christian witness who had faced death threats when his white Baptist church in Durham, North Carolina, had welcomed blacks in the same year that the 16th St. Baptist Church was bombed in Birmingham. Yet this preacher did not announce to me the tired tidings of moral effort. He did not tell me to become socially and politically righteous. He declared the unsurpassably Good News that all the sophistication and morality in the world would not save me or anyone else. My only hope, he declared, was the world's only hope: salvation by God's grace alone through the gift of faith alone in Jesus Christ.[8]

The best guarantor of our hearing difficult questions put to us by others is the gospel of Jesus Christ. This is hard for us to believe because we think that in order to hear another we must first lay aside our faith and engage the stranger at some "higher" level. We must, so to speak, "move beyond faith." When we do that, however, what is lost is the difficulty of the questions. They became spiritualized and therefore easier, a matter for our private selves to determine. Or they become politicized, no more a matter of truth but simply a question of power. In either case, we are freed from having to *listen* to the questions as questions addressed to us. We do not even have to *see* the person asking the questions. We are unentangled, unrelated to the other who, we are convinced, has no real claim on us. By setting aside our faith in Jesus Christ we are setting aside the community that Christ has made through his cross. Life in this community reveals that even our "enemies" have a claim on us and it is to their questions we must attend, for whatever else they are, they are not enemies to Christ.

That, of course, is what Ralph Wood discovered when Zuma Allen looked at him, and when a Roman Catholic teacher challenged his faith, and when a Baptist preacher wrestled him for his soul. The faith he had been taught as a child made their questions more pressing, more difficult to avoid, more embarrassing to live with. He did not need a course in pluralism to get him out from under the bed. Indeed, a course in pluralism would never have put him under the bed in the first place. All he needed to feel the full force of Zuma Allen's withering look was the gospel contained in the lyric, "Red and yellow, black and white, they are precious in his sight. Jesus loves the little children of the world." That gospel makes the questions of our "enemies" difficult enough.

But it is also that gospel that makes us take our "enemies" seriously. There is a kind of pluralism that seeks to include all by dismissing all, that maintains that all assertions of the truth are the same because the truth is unknowable. Such a nihilistic "openness" reflects a deep loss of nerve within our own culture, but one of its truly insidious effects is the way in which such a pluralism gives permission to folk simply to dismiss the convictions of those with whom we disagree. Nothing could be more patronizing or even closed than such "openness."

But in calling us to "love our enemies," Jesus does them the favor of taking what they believe seriously. He does not deny them the dignity of being opposed to him, even doing so in the name of some conviction he seeks to overthrow. The New Testament is full of folk to whom Jesus extends this dignity: to his own disciples, to Nicodemus, to the Pharisees. What he does not ever seem to do is to say, "Well, it really doesn't matter. Who can know the truth anyway? If you want to believe that way, it's up to you." No, he hears their questions, suffers their opposition, even grows angry with their hardness of heart, or refusal to understand, all the while paying them the high compliment of engaging them in the matter of the truth.

It has been the argument of this chapter that such an engagement cannot be sustained apart from faith in the one who calls us to "love our enemies." That we fail here, as elsewhere, is hardly a surprise, but that we do so serves only to remind us that our need of grace is great and we do not rid ourselves of such need by "moving beyond faith." Like any good sermon, the Christian life only takes a miracle to be believed, just as it takes miracle after miracle to be lived. If it came any easier, then we would not need the Holy Spirit either to believe or to live.

3

The Arrogance of Modesty
and the End of Autonomy

"What I like about teaching theology here is the diversity
of the student body and the openness and freedom we have
as faculty in addressing the issues of the day in a variety of
ways."[1] What could be less offensive than such a statement?
It is modest and unassuming and it celebrates the unnarrow
life of a community dedicated to the quest for understanding.
Yet William Willimon, who cites this quotation (taken from
an ad inviting students to consider a seminary), concludes
that as such, it represents "a succinct statement of what is
wrong with seminary teaching today."[2]

Willimon thinks that such a celebration of opennesss and
diversity, though apparently modest in its claims concerning
the truth of the faith, is nevertheless arrogant in its certainty
of self and in its contentment with the surrounding culture. In
contrast, he offers the experience of a colleague of his who
taught on the Protestant Faculty at Yaounde in Cameroon,
where African students, whose original language was not even
the language of instruction (i.e., French), spent their first year
learning Hebrew and Greek and over the next three years were
required to take at least one theology course presupposing the
original languages. Willimon concludes: "I suspect that the
Africans have a greater sense that the church is confronting a
major adversary than we do. If one looks at the preponderance
of therapeutically rather than theologically based courses in
our curricula, we appear to be preparing students for a career
of helping people adjust to the dilemmas of their affluence."[3]

But who could oppose openness or diversity? Who would even want to do that, especially in the name of the Christian faith? Is following Jesus Christ supposed to make us narrower people? Is that what the gospel is after?

By no means! But Willimon, along with many others, has learned to be suspicious of certain words, even words as desirable as "openness" and "diversity," not because he is against such things but because he knows that the meaning of such terms is not self-evident. Words are tricky things and their meanings are determined by the central narrative that authorizes and informs their particular use. The central narrative authorizing and informing the use of words in the training of gospel ministers is, presumably, the narrative of the gospel itself. If the meaning of our words is not determined in the light of that central story, they become empty words, words that can all too easily be filled in accordance with other authorities. As a result, when we use such words uncritically—that is, without reference to the gospel's story—they can easily mean just the opposite of what we might think. George Orwell has taught us how easy it is for principalities and powers within any particular culture to make "war" be understood as "peace," and "love" to be read as "hate." Words reflect the "powers" that authorize them. Moreover, the perversion of words rarely comes in something obviously evil or wrong, but in the guise of what appears to be good and virtuous, in words that any "right-thinking person" should approve.

Willimon thinks that most students who come to college or university or seminary today are more shaped by the culture and its use of words than by the church and its tradition. The story they believe in might be called "the Enlightenment story" or the "story of modernity." It is a story that has assured them that they are autonomous creatures who have been formed by no particular tradition or faith and who are answerable only to themselves. Accordingly, they are to attend primarily to their own opinions and experience, which are weightier matters than the tradition of the church and its history of confessing the faith. As one might imagine, such a "cultural story" tends to make its adherents "modest" about claims that exceed the authority of their own experience or opinions.

Like many others, however, Willimon recognizes that such "modesty" is rooted in an unexamined if not arrogant "certitude of self." This starting point is itself part of a long tradition and deserves at least as much scrutiny as the tradition it seeks to criticize. For example, it is a peculiarly modern notion that we are autonomous individuals who have access to some kind of pure rationality unfettered by connections to locale or history, a rationality that is then able to pass judgment on embodied traditions of apprehending and expressing the truth. Of course, this was precisely the claim of the Enlightenment: the discovery and appropriate use of "pure reason." In more recent years, however, the pursuit of "pure reason," that is, a reason untainted by history or personal faith or gender or race or a hundred other entangling commitments, has proved elusive. Indeed, the notion of "pure reason" has itself proved to be an illusion, for the only reason available to us is that which comes in socially embodied forms and is borne to us through historical traditions of reasoning.[4] So the tradition that claims to honor no tradition is itself a tradition that shapes how we think. Or to put it another way, we are unable to think without thinking within a tradition of some kind. So the question becomes not, "Will a tradition determine how I think?" It will, of necessity. Rather, the question becomes, "Will the tradition that determines how I think be faithful to Christ and his church?"[5] That is the decisive question that confessing Christ in a pluralistic culture has to answer.

Willimon offers a final example of how "modesty" in the face of the gospel's claims often rests on a smug contentment with ourselves and sometimes even with an arrogant refusal to have to depend upon another in the matter of faith. He recalls that in his own days as a seminary student, an Orthodox priest was invited to lecture on the development of the creeds. At the end of the lecture, one of the students asked Father Theodore what he should do when he finds it impossible to affirm certain tenets of the creed.

> The priest look confused. "Well, you just say it. It's not that hard to master. With a little effort, most can learn it by heart."

"No, you don't understand," continued the student, "what am I to do when I have difficulty affirming parts of the creed—like the Virgin Birth?"

The priest continued to look confused. "You just say it. Particularly when you have difficulty believing it, you just keep saying it. It will come to you eventually."

Exasperatedly, the student . . . pleaded, "How can I with integrity affirm a creed in which I do not believe?"

"It's not *your* creed, young man!" said the priest. "It's *our* creed. Keep saying it, for heaven's sake! Eventually, it may come to you. For some, it takes longer than for others. How old are you? Twenty-three? Don't be so hard on yourself. There are lots of things that one doesn't know at 23. Eventually, it may come to you. Even if it doesn't, don't worry. It's not *your* creed."[6]

Willimon concludes: "At that moment I realized what was wrong with much of the education I received. A light shone. . . . I thanked God that, in my ministry, I was not being left to my own devices. I did not have to think for myself. Saints led the way."[7]

For a culture whose tradition has been to honor no tradition, the notion of having to rely on saints to lead the way may not come as particularly good news. For Willimon it constituted freedom from self, that is, freedom from the arrogant cultural presumption that unless I confirm it, the truth of the faith is not established. It is presumptuous precisely because it presumes that the Christian faith is finally about "me," a presumption that our culture needs very little encouragement in believing. Indeed, such a presumption is a vital part of American piety. "He walks with me and he talks with me, and he tells me I am his own," we sing, and then, even more blasphemously, though no less cheerfully, "and the joy we share as we tarry there, none other has ever known." None other, just Jesus and me.

All of which makes it very difficult for us to understand or appreciate scripture and its strange story of the church, and of God's choosing of Israel, and of election itself. If God wants to communicate something to me, then surely God will "walk with me and talk with me and tell me I am his own." Why would I need

Israel? Why the church? Why, when you come right down to it, would I need scripture or the confessions or even Jesus Christ? God can talk to me directly, can he not?

Such questions imply that when it comes to faith we are all "free agents," that is, independent individuals who do not have to rely on "saints," much less on certain disciplines or practices to lead the Christian life. To be sure, we might be in need of an example or a good teacher, but a really good teacher, one like Socrates, succeeds in the end by making himself superfluous, by training us for autonomy. The notion that we need a teacher whose teaching we can never dispense with but upon whom we must rely to begin afresh again and again, that notion is offensive to us. It suggests that we are not the autonomous creatures we like to think we are, but rather we are creatures who are made for relationship and who depend on that relationship for our life. That, in fact, is the way scripture views human life: not as a set of autonomous individuals disconnected from the vagaries of time and space, but in terms of human relationships that are bound up with family and tribe and home. As the Genesis story makes clear, full humanity is always cohumanity ("So God created humankind in his image, . . . male and female he created them" [Gen. 1:27]). Until Eve is created, Adam's humanity is deficient ("This at last is bone of my bones and flesh of my flesh" [Gen. 2:23]).

Their story unfolds as first of all the story of man and woman, and then of parents and children, and finally tribes and nations. As Lesslie Newbigin notes:

> This mutual relatedness, this dependence of one on another, is not merely part of the journey toward the goal of salvation, but is intrinsic to the goal itself. For knowing God, for being in communion with him, we are dependent on the one whom he gives us to be the bearer of this relation, not just as a teacher and guide on the way but as the partner in the end. There is, there can be, no private salvation, no salvation which does not involve us with one another.[8]

Indeed, in order to receive God's gift of salvation, we must receive the neighbor who bears it to us.

The formal name for the strange way scripture speaks of God's saving revelation through the mediation of others is the doctrine of election. It is through God's election of Israel that all the nations will be blessed, as the original promise to Abraham indicated. It is through God's engrafting of Gentiles into this promise that the church is elected in Christ. And above all, it is in Jesus Christ himself that God elects this world for love and praise and joy, just as it is in Jesus Christ that God rejects all that would bring this world to nothing.

Whatever we might think of the doctrine of election, it has the virtue of keeping God's redemptive grace at the center of the gospel's story. This story is not about America. It is not, at least in the first instance, even about "me" and my "spirituality." It is about the strange God who saves this world in the oddest way, through the Jew, Jesus Christ, whose life is itself mediated in history through Israel and the church. This is not the way we would have done things, for this way forces us to depend on the witness of Israel and the church, to live not only with the Jewishness of Jesus but also with our never-ending need of his presence. And worse, this way results in our having to receive Jesus not privately or "in the garden" by myself or through some cosmic illumination, but in the company of those whom he has chosen not to be without, the prophets and apostles, the sinners and saints of his church.

This way of doing business is scandalous, never more so than in its even more scandalous insistence that the truth of the whole universe is embedded in the story of this one man, Jesus Christ. How could that be in a world where "pure reason" dictates that there is no special place, no special time, no special person to which one or some are granted access to the truth and others must find themselves forever dependent? How could that be in a world where there are many founders of a religion, some of whose teachings put Christians to shame in the wisdom and devotion and generosity of their adherents? Yet nothing less than just such a scandalous claim is what the church confesses when it confesses Jesus Christ as Lord. And just so do we confront the full scandal of having to be saved by a mysterious grace not of our own choosing, a grace that saves us by rendering us dependent upon others. For it is just such a grace that this strange God employs to save Gentiles through the life of a Jew, and yet will not allow Gentiles to confess the faith apart from the election of Israel. Instead of privileging one group over another, this gospel unrelentingly describes a mutual need, the strange "logic of election"[9] that invites us to receive the gospel from the people Jesus sticks us with.

That is what it means to be stuck with Christ, namely, to be stuck with what belongs to Christ. If we think about that for a moment, we can readily see that to be stuck with Christ does not bring with it some privileged status. Christ died with two bandits on the cross. He died abandoned by his disciples, mocked by the leaders of his faith, indifferently executed by the political authorities. It is not too strong to say that for the elite within his own culture, he died as a nobody, yet another lost cause, a troublesome rabble-rouser, a confused holy man. That Christians today should question why bad things happen to such nice people like us is only possible if we have forgotten Jesus' story and think that his followers should be immune from such suffering. He was not; why should his followers be? Indeed, election in scripture is never perceived as an unmitigated blessing. Jonah would have been just as happy if God had called someone else to go to Nineveh; Job certainly would have been pleased if God had picked someone else for "Exhibit A" in human faithfulness; Jeremiah even accuses God of tricking him, seducing him, and making him a laughingstock (Jer. 20:7). The author of Hebrews concludes: "Others suffered mocking and flogging, and even chains and imprisonment. They were stoned, they were sawn in two, they were killed by the sword. . . . destitute, persecuted, tormented—of whom the world was not worthy. They wandered in deserts and mountains, and in caves and holes in the ground" (Heb. 11:36–38). Election means being chosen to share in Christ's mission, and therefore in Christ's sufferings, even being baptized into the historically embodied tradition that is constituted by his life and bears his message to the world. Election means being formed into Christ's own life.

Though we often protest that any notion of election offends our democratic sensibilities, one wonders if it is not this doctrine's uncompromising memory of what the gospel story is about that really offends us. An affluent culture is a master at hiding from us our dependence upon and even need of others, and we resent the reminder that we are in need at all, much less in need of someone we have not chosen. Moreover, our affluence has a way of making us more "spiritual."

But even so, it is not just our resentments that make the notion of election difficult. Just as some have used this teaching to elevate themselves to a privileged status, so others have accepted the notion of suffering and endurance while assuming that such will give them some eventual claim on God. Paul demolishes that assumption when he reminds the Gentiles in the Roman church that if they, "a wild olive shoot," were engrafted into Israel's life to share in the promise to Abraham, they are not to be proud. "For if God did not spare the natural branches, perhaps he will not spare you" (Rom. 11:21). No, all there is room for here is wonder, love, and praise. There is no reason to boast. "For God has imprisoned all in disobedience so that he may be merciful to all" (Rom. 11:32).

That is how the cross makes community in a broken and splintered world: first by relentlessly exposing our opposition to grace, revealing us to be a community of sinners, and then by naming us as the recipients of that grace, claiming us as the community of the forgiven. As the community of the cross, the church is that socially embodied form of the gospel that is not ashamed of living out its faith amidst all the ambiguities of history. Just so does it embody the hope that points to the end of history, to that community of the Lamb where the nations will be healed and God will wipe away every tear.

Baptism as a Denial of Self-Invention

This chapter began by noting that there is no truth available to us that exists independently of history, of such entangling factors as race or gender or location or even faith commitment. However, one of the great goals of the Enlightenment faith was to enable people to believe in God without their having to accept such limitations, that is, without having to deal with something as messy and as historically tainted as the church and its claims. Deism had a certain attraction for just this reason. It kept things neat. One could be a believer in a generic god without having to make historical claims or participate in the practices or institutions of a particular tradition. After all, such a deity could remain in heaven, simply starting the world as if it were a watch, and then letting it run its course. But such a neat view had its price. That price had to do with a kind of denial of history, a claim that history's temporally bound truths could never be anything more than just that—temporally bound. They could never be the basis for anything so substantial as faith in God.[10] Accordingly, as God became more "spiritual" and even ideal, history became strangely diminished, hopeless even. All the important questions lay elsewhere: the purpose of history, its end and goal, the nature of a human life—these questions could not be answered from within history. They could only be answered from "beyond history," from those timeless truths that "reason" or "faith" might intuit or discern.

But such answers, divorced from temporal events, could only evacuate history of any overarching or ultimate meaning, throwing us back on ourselves to construct our own meanings. To be sure, just such a vacuum is what we have come to think of as the very definition of freedom: the pursuit of an unspecified happiness. "Be what you want to be," we are told. "Imagine a world without limits," a commercial suggests. And so we do, and then are surprised when a world of unlimited self-invention proves profoundly lethal to such historically fragile things as families, marriages, friendships, neighborhoods, schools, and even the church itself.

In contrast, the God whose truth is revealed in history, in and through Israel, the church, and preeminently in the incarnation of Jesus Christ, is the God who has time for us, who takes our time and our limits seriously. This is what it means that the Word became flesh. The unfolding of God's revelation is inseparable from particular events and specific places: Hebron, Egypt, Sinai, Canaan, Jericho, Bethlehem, Jerusalem. Such places are not "spiritual" centers where individuals are put in touch with some timeless deity, but, rather, they are stations on a long journey that this God undertakes in history with those whom he has chosen to disclose his purpose. As Paul summarizes the gospel for the church gathered in Rome, the gift of life in Jesus Christ is not a piece of "pure reason" that helps us escape the vicissitudes of time and space, but it is the process of being engrafted into the story of a particular people, of being made heirs of a particular promise, of being adopted as children of a covenant that compels us to remember and to hope. There is in this story a celebration of the mundane, the happy embrace of the ordinary, the numbering of days as a mark of wisdom. This story invites us to take our daily lives seriously, as if each day really were a gift from the God who has time for us.

Who we are, then, is not up to our imagining or reimagining, much less to our ability to escape history, but is a function of our being embraced within history by the God who has already revealed the plot of this narrative in the life, death, and resurrection of Jesus Christ. It is that embrace the church celebrates in the sacrament of Baptism, a sacrament that tells us we are free from the terrible burden of self-invention. We are not left to the tender mercies of the culture. We have a story. We have a past. We have a future. And these things, far from threatening our "happiness," are the very things that enable us to enter into history fully, to receive the gift of our days not as some prison we must seek to escape but as the blessing of the ordinary, the daily gift of life in Christ.

Self-invention, of course, is the great task of a culture that denies that God has entered history. In the absence of God's purpose, we must supply our own, we think. Such a task, however, assumes that our souls are infinitely plastic things that can be shaped and fitted to what the culture requires. Even more, it assumes that we who are doing this shaping exist somehow above history, that there is an "I" untainted by the limitations of space and time. When this task becomes politicized, what is created is a totalitarian state that seeks to make a "new man" or "new woman" of some kind. And if individuals prove not sufficiently plastic, they will be required to take a course in "reeducation," a place for the incorrigibles to be reinvented, forcibly if need be. Failing that, their images can simply be effaced; they can become "nonpersons."

However, even in a consumer society that celebrates the individual's rights, we become no less interested in self-creation and in some ways prove more lethal in our efforts. We engage in "makeovers," ceaselessly yearning for "a new me," and always confident that we can keep our options open. Yet our makeovers never quite succeed, just as our pursuit of happiness, divorced from the entanglements of time and place and obligation, becomes an increasingly lonely and desperate business. Our freedom to invent ourselves turns out to be not much of a freedom at all, but just another kind of self-constructed hell, a way we seek to hide from God's intrusive love.

Self-invention has become for our culture the primary way of avoiding the claims of the gospel. Nowhere is this more true than in that religious form of self-invention, in which "repentance" becomes the religious equivalent of yet another makeover. That is why it has become a devalued word in our culture, why it appears so cheap. "Repentance" appears to hold out the possibility of a new invention of self, a self unburdened by the past and free now to begin with a clean slate. "Lighting out for the territory" has always been the American way, and often the "repentance" popular religion celebrates is but another way of assuring ourselves that we are still at the center of our own stories, unconstrained by any past we have not chosen. By reducing "repentance" to yet another form of self-invention, we declare that history really has no meaning, that the "I" who did that wicked thing yesterday is not the "real me," just as who "I" will be tomorrow is a matter of my own choosing. One simply "moves on." Religion has often proved useful in this way.

However, here the gospel cuts most deeply by speaking of baptism in terms of dying and rising. That is the regular course of the Christian life, not improving every day in every way into a "new me," but a dying and rising in Christ, in which I am displaced. Something of me dies. That sinful person who always seeks a self-constructed reality apart from the cross of Jesus Christ is judged and condemned. And that same sinful person who is judged and condemned is buried with Christ in his tomb and raised to a life where Christ is the center. What constitutes our dying and rising is not some ecstatic experience or yet another makeover but Christ's death and our being raised into Christ's life. Whatever life we live from here on, we live by faith in him. It is not a new "me" then, that is at the center. Indeed, "it is no longer I who live, but it is Christ who lives in me" (Gal. 2:20). "Do you not know that all of us who have been baptized into Christ Jesus were baptized into his death? Therefore we have been buried with him by baptism into death, so that, just as Christ was raised from the dead by the glory of the Father, so we too might walk in newness of life" (Rom. 6:3).

This is the happy exchange that the gospel brings about. To be baptized is to come to the end of "me" and the whole effort of self-invention. All of that is seen to be unreal, and all of that dies on the cross. In its place we are raised to real life, to a life "hidden with Christ in God" (Col. 3:3). In this sense, baptism is a statement about reality. To understand "me" or you or anyone now, we must look first to Christ and his story, for there is where reality begins; there God has told the truth about our lives, revealing us to be creatures who are made for communion with him. In Christ we are baptized into a life of communion, into the life that participates through the Holy Spirit in the incarnate Son's communion with the Father. The messiness of history, far from becoming a hindrance to such participation, becomes, rather, the very stuff out of which the triune God creates the communion of the saints in Christ. Indeed, here the sacrament of baptism testifies to God's initiative throughout, for even before we are capable of thinking about inventing ourselves or escaping history, God enters our lives and through the gift of the Holy Spirit enables us to participate in the incarnate Son's own life. The words of the French Reformed baptismal service make this point beautifully. Over the child, the pastor says:

> Little child, for you Jesus Christ has come, he has fought, he has suffered. For you he entered the shadow of Gethsemane and the horror of Calvary. For you he uttered the cry, "It is finished!" For you he rose from the dead and ascended into heaven and there he intercedes—for you, little child, even though you do not know it. But in this way the word of the Gospel becomes true. "We love him, because he first loved us."[11]

Baptism does not merely redeem the past. It also grants a future. "The old man dies," writes Bonhoeffer, "but it is God who has conquered him. Now we share in the resurrection of Christ and eternal life."[12]

What does that mean? No doubt it can be described in a number of ways, but surely in our day it is best described in terms of hope. To share in the life of the risen Lord must mean more than just "happiness" or even "joy." It must mean something like a hope that risks being embodied in communities of faith, in communities that consciously resist the nothingness that our culture regularly deals out by affirming instead life together in Jesus Christ. To hope is to worship and celebrate that life together in him. It is to be the church amidst the messiness of history, risking the public exposure of our own faith because we are confident in him who meets us precisely in such messiness and there forms us into his own humanity.

What does such hope look like? What is the life we are baptized into? It would be easy to glamorize the life of the church. Anybody, however, who participates in its life regularly would know how false such a picture is. But just as the cross gives us a past and a future, so does being baptized into Christ give us a hope-shaped community in which to practice the gift of hope. Here, as the story is retold and the narrative rehearsed, we are given eyes to see what we would otherwise have overlooked: the world that God loves, the world we are invited to embrace for Jesus' sake. The church may not look like much, but ordinary congregations are the way the Holy Spirit chooses to form saints in the world, to draw us into that newness of life that alone is strong enough to love the world. That is why to hope for this world has always meant to commit evangelism, that is, it has always meant loving the world enough to contend for the truth that all human beings are made for communion with God. Even more than that, it has meant to contend for this truth not by arguing for it but by being formed into communities of worship and praise.

Sometimes it is all that we can do simply to affirm our faith, to say, "Yes, I believe in God." Sometimes it is even more than we can do. But the hope contained in such words, the "vigorous assertion of personal dignity"[13] that such words affirm in insisting that we are created for life with God, shakes our culture to its very foundations. A young woman of seventeen in Littleton, Colorado, filled with anxieties about her weight and popularity, went to school one day and said, "Yes, I believe in God," to a fellow student holding a gun to her head. She was killed. In the midst of the tragedy and loss and the ultimate trivializing of life that took place that day, her words may seem nothing more than a whisper. Nevertheless, her "vigorous assertion of personal dignity," rooted in Christ and formed by saints, enabled her to take herself far more seriously than a culture scrupulously modest about any such claims. She believed in God and found in that affirmation not a leisurely openness and freedom in addressing issues in a variety of ways, but a dangerously liberating truth that contradicted her culture's deepest affirmations and may well have cost her her life. By saying Yes, she made the outrageous claim that she was in fact a gift, a claim a culture bent on its own self-inventiveness could not abide. But her words of faith have become a blessing to many. Like that of the martyrs of old, her witness has itself been a gift of deep encouragement to a culture all too ready to move on. For she has invited us to stop and dare with her to speak the truth, to affirm that we too are gifts, fearfully and wonderfully made, not to be disposed of or simply consumed but to live in the praise of the eternally rich God. As a preacher in one of Flannery O'Connor's stories says to a child he has just baptized, "You count now."[14] And so we do.

This chapter began by casting doubt on the modesty of a culture in which questions of faith are trivialized in the name of a presumed autonomy. It ends with the wonderfully immodest affirmation of faith, "Yes, I believe in God." The one constant theme throughout has been the conviction that the Christian life is being in communion, that it participates in a life deeper than our own. The name for that life is the Trinity, the communion of Father, Son, and Holy Spirit. To that life we now turn.

4

Trinitarian Life

*T*here are times, Fred Craddock says, when you can hear from the center of reality a groan.[1] It is not the kind of groan that we make when we lift something too heavy or stare at an unweeded garden. It is deeper than that, almost a sigh, almost as if what we want to say cannot be put into words.

She had been dying of cancer for a long time. A beautiful woman whose beauty the disease was slowly ravaging, she had mercifully retained her vanity even in the face of drastic weight loss and numerous surgeries. Her lovely blonde hair had been poisoned out of her by the chemotherapy, but she had purchased a wig that she insisted on wearing even in bed. I had been her pastor for ten years, and during that time we had worked together on the session, on building committees, and on presbytery events. More than that, we had partied together, celebrated victories, mourned losses, laughed at each other and the world. I had buried her mother and officiated at her daughter's wedding. Now she was dying.

She had asked me to come to her home and bring Communion to her and her family. So I went with an elder in our church who had prepared the bread and the wine, and we entered her bedroom. Her husband was there, as well as her sister and her children and some neighbors and friends. As I prayed the prayers and broke the bread, I began to hear her groaning. It was more like a whimper really, a sigh, an inarticulate longing. I looked at her and asked her if she wanted me to continue and she nodded her head. But her groaning embarrassed me.

I was there as her pastor, I thought. I was there to do something for her, to perform a ritual, perhaps a palliative act of kindness, to offer some dignified way of acknowledging this dying. As I read the words of institution (". . . that the Lord Jesus on the night when he was betrayed took bread, and when he had given thanks he broke it, and said, 'This is my body which is for you. Do this in remembrance of me'") and handed her a piece of bread, I called her by name and invited her to take and eat, for just so she would proclaim the saving death of the risen Lord until he comes again. She took the bread and sipped the wine and said nothing. But she continued to groan.

It was not the first time. There is a woman in our congregation who had a stroke at a very young age. The stroke paralyzed her on her left side and rendered her utterly inarticulate. All she can do is groan. Sometimes she groans with a complaint; often she groans in delight. Every Sunday she worships with us and sits in her wheelchair almost beneath the pulpit. It is a fearful thing to preach to one whose groans are as eloquent and as moving as hers. When she takes Communion, she waits eagerly for the help she needs to take the bread and the cup to her lips.

Paul writes that all of creation groans, and that we ourselves "groan inwardly" as we await "the redemption of our bodies" (Rom. 8:23) Was that why my friend was groaning, whose body was wasted with cancer? Is that what I hear on Sunday morning when from a wheelchair there comes this deep sigh? Maybe it is not so far removed from an unweeded garden, for there are times when we long for something better, something more beautiful. The Holy Spirit only seems to make matters worse, for, as Craddock notes, it is the Spirit who not only quickens our hope for a new creation but also intensifies the pain we feel over the difference between the way things are and the way things ought to be.[2] That longing for beauty, for wholeness, for righteousness always sounds like a groan, and it is the stuff of both our songs of lament and our cries for justice.

Gathering around a dying woman to celebrate Communion has a way of introducing us to reality. There we can hear the groans. Sometimes it is difficult to do so on Sunday morning, when we are dressed in our Sunday best and are enjoying good health and prosperity. Then we run the risk of being impressed with our fullness, of being under the illusion that worship is a "groanless" affair, something that we do with beautiful music and entertaining words, rather than something in which we participate. Then we almost need to be interrupted by someone else's groaning to realize where we are and why we have come. Such groans testify against a culture that would trivialize our lives into something merely presentable. Listening to my dying friend groan reminded me how little worship is something that we do and how much it is something that we receive, a life in which we participate, a dance in which we lose ourselves, a meal in which we are invited to share.

Celebrating the Lord's Supper with a dying woman may seem a strange way to begin talking about the triune God, but in fact the very groans we hear echo God's own groaning. "Likewise the Spirit helps us in our weakness; for we do not know how to pray as we ought, but that very Spirit intercedes with sighs too deep for words" (Rom. 8:26). What had brought that Communion to the bedside of a dying woman was love, the love of the triune God for her. That love had groaned once on the cross and so became present to her now, not leaving her with some mere memory but claiming her time and her place in the triune terms of its own life of Good Friday, Easter, and Pentecost. God's love for her was not ashamed or embarrassed by her groaning. With "sighs too deep for words," God's Spirit took her sighs and made of her life a prayer that was wholly articulate and dauntingly beautiful. So did she, out of her last need, proclaim the death of the risen Lord until he comes.

But just so was her life seen in Trinitarian terms, God the Spirit interceding for her with the God who in Jesus Christ takes our time and place seriously and who finds in the messy, temporal, and geographically bound life she lived just the right stuff out of which to do his redeeming work. Unlike the gods we create who promise to liberate us from the confines of history, the triune God does not seem to be embarrassed by locale; even the groans of a dying woman do not seem to be insuperable to him. A few days before she died, this woman celebrated the life that was hers in a small town in Texas, a life that she had found in the life, death, and resurrection of Jesus Christ.

God is love, which means that God groans. There is no love without this groaning. Paul suggests that this groaning is but the labor pains of a new creation God is bringing about. Such groaning is at one with Jesus' own cries, the cries he utters in the face of human hurt (e.g., Mark 7:34) or rejection (e.g., Mark 8:11) or his own cry of dereliction (e.g., Mark 15:34, 37). If the groans we utter while receiving bread and wine mean anything, surely they indicate a sharing in Christ's own life, a participation, however inadequate or incomplete, in that humanity which in Christ is offered to the Father in the Spirit, and through which we come to know what it is to be human. In this sense, Jesus Christ is the real agent in our worship, our "high priest," as the book of Hebrews insists (Heb. 9:11). Here too we follow him. But here too his self-giving mediates to us a life in a particular place, a sharing in the life of God in a particular community. Communion then is not an individual's effort to transcend the limitations of time and place, but it is our sharing in the locale of the triune God, in the life together given to us in Jesus Christ. This sharing, this *koinonia*, this communion describes God's own life as a life of mutuality and love, not a solitary life but a life of relatedness, a life that can hear the groans.

That is why, as James Torrance has suggested, we are never more truly human than when we sit at the Lord's Table, "when Christ draws us into his life of communion with the Father and into communion with one another."[3] This is the great promise of Christian worship, for here we feed on him and so receive our humanity as we "lift up our hearts unto the Lord." Here we receive the mysterious gift of a life that is made for communion, indeed, a life that reflects in our very creatureliness ("male and female he created them" [Gen. 1:27]) the image of God's own self-relatedness. Here we do not lose our individuality in some massive collectivity anymore than we preserve our isolation in some lonely struggle to save our own souls. To be a person, rather, is to be someone who has "come home" to this table; it is to be someone who has at last "come to himself" (Luke 15:17), and has found his true place in communion with others in his Father's house.

That is not the usual way we think of ourselves. We are much more comfortable thinking of ourselves as "jealous gods" bristling with rights, or as consumers busily realizing ourselves. We contract to come together for certain specified purposes, but there is no covenant that really holds us together. Before long we find our lives trivialized into ever smaller rivulets of self. Seeing others either as potential rivals or as existing only to meet "my needs," we find there is no mutual giving or receiving, no offering of self, no intimacy of shared communion. Indeed, we claim to find such notions confining even as the triviality and loneliness of our own lives become more and more apparent. Hoping to render ourselves more significant, we can only dream of escaping the confines of time and place, projecting our longing for timelessness onto God, as if by doing so we might commune with him more "spiritually," unfettered by the impediments of the flesh. Just so is all the groaning, all the messy, historical stuff of life discarded and we are left to imagine or reimagine much less embarrassing ways of thinking about God, ways that will allow us to escape the scandalous presence of God in the flesh of Jesus Christ. Yet it is that scandalous presence that keeps us from despising what is ordinary, from holding in contempt something as ridiculous as the church, from despairing over our neighbors or the smallness of our own lives.

Our embarrassment over the groaning is nothing more than our embarrassment with Christ's own humanity. The gospel has always been scandalous in this way. The triune life of the God revealed in Jesus Christ is rich in such groanings, just as it is relentless in its embrace of time and place, wholly unembarrassed to come to us *in the flesh*. In the life broken and poured out around the Lord's Table, the fleshliness of the risen Lord becomes the very means of our discovering a mutuality of love that subverts all our "rights" and surprises all our "certainties." That is how the Spirit intercedes for us, not only in completing our prayers with sighs too deep for words, but also by drawing us into communion with the real presence of Jesus Christ such that we are no longer ashamed of the groaning, no longer ashamed to find ourselves in this time and place surround by the company of others, at his table.

Fred Craddock tells of hearing Albert Schweitzer groan and how such a groan subverted Craddock's desire to render a timeless judgment on a man's life, revealing to him instead the much more daunting prospect of loving a particular people in a particular time and place for Jesus' sake. After preparing himself to ask Schweitzer a series of questions at an appearance at a local church, Craddock, a young seminarian at the time, writes:

> I rushed downstairs to sit on the front row of the chairs assembled there, and there was punch and there were cookies and there were peanuts. Oh, and we ate and nibbled and we drank a bit and waited for his appearance. Finally he came with a cup of tea. He was about seventy-five years old. His hair was white and long. His mustache was bushy. . . . I had my questions—surely there would be question/answer time. He got up and said, "I thank you for your hospitality, for your gracious reception of me, but I have to go back to Lambarene in Africa. My people are dying there. They are sick and they are hungry. If any of you have in you the love of Jesus, come help me." I looked at my questions. Of all the stupid silly stuff that I was going to ask this man, who stood in front of us, and groaned.[4]

The threat that confronts the church today is the trivialization of its own faith by a culture all too willing to assimilate the claims of that faith into some other purpose. That is to say, we will do almost anything to avoid hearing the groaning, even to the point of retreating into a spirituality of our own devising, into a spirituality unmarked by the Word made flesh. But as Craddock makes clear, it is precisely the life of the triune God incarnate in Jesus Christ that compels us to hear the groans of those who are in our very midst, to hear the groans of those even in Lambarene as the groans of "our people." "If any of you have in you the love of Jesus, come help me." That is a call to a particular place. It is not a call to settle some universal question once and for all. Rather, it is an invitation to love a particular place and a particular people for Jesus' sake. Indeed, it is an invitation to enter the Trinitarian terms of God's being in communion, the life made known to us in Jesus Christ. We do not have to go to Lambarene to respond to this call, but we will not be able to know the triune God without hearing the groaning.

The One, the Three, and the Many

When we think of God, we think more easily in unitarian terms than we do in Trinitarian terms. This is partly due to the fact that we live in the West and are not used to thinking of God in terms of threeness. But it is also due to the fact that we have learned to think of God not so much in terms of the way we receive him in Jesus Christ but in terms of our idea of what God should be like. The medieval age thought of God in terms of "Being itself," and so spoke of God more and more abstractly in terms of certain perfections. An "unmoved Mover," God was that One around whom the universe revolved. Even the Enlightenment did not challenge this understanding of God, but thought of God as "the Clockmaker" or even as some more abstract deity, largely disengaged from the day to day affairs of the universe. When asked by Napoleon at the beginning of the nineteenth century where God was in his theory of celestial mechanics, La Place famously replied that he had no need of that hypothesis. The God whose love would intrude upon our world came to be perceived as a threat to our freedom. Indeed, it is a sign of modernity to try to think without God.

Such efforts to think without God should not offend us. In some ways, they represent an understandable reaction against an earlier theology that presumed to explain too much. The Bible is not about everything. If it is used for purposes that have nothing to do with the promise it unfolds, then it loses its authority, and the resulting biology or paleontology or even theology based on it will only bring ridicule to its believers. "Dare to think" was the battle cry of the Enlightenment, given to it by one of its greatest philosophers, Immanuel Kant, who himself could only find room for God as a means of bolstering up our morality. Yet the god whom Kant and so many others found oppressive was not the triune God revealed in Jesus Christ whose Spirit gathers us into communities of faith. That God baffled the philosophers of the Enlightenment and could, they thought, safely be dismissed. No, the god from whose presence they sought relief was the "One" whom Emerson found so oppressive and who could only be dealt with by displacing him with the thinking individual.

The Westminster Shorter Catechism defines this "One" in its question 6: "What is God?" We might well think that a strange question to ask, as if God were a thing. In any case, the answer given is: "God is a Spirit, infinite, eternal, unchangeable in his being wisdom, justice, goodness and truth." In some ways this answer seems comprehensive enough, but the being it describes appears to be more of an abstraction than anything else, a piling up of virtues and powers. Moreover, it leaves out a good deal. Here is a divine being whose life can be described apart from Jesus Christ, a being who can be defined even without reference to love. Can such a being hear the groans? Here is a "One" who can only appear oppressive to the "many." And if it is the case that this One governs the world not through communion with us in Jesus Christ but through "eternal decrees," then this One can only appear to be a kind of tyrant. Just as the modern world can be characterized politically by its impatience with absolutist regimes in which the one (the king) oppresses the many, so a theology of an absolutist deity was overthrown in the name of a kinder "Creator" ("Nature" and "Nature's God") who, having endowed us with certain inalienable rights, had the good grace to abdicate the stage and leave us pretty much to our own devices. The One was excluded from the modern world, displaced by the many in the name of freedom or "pure reason" or "self-evidence." That the many might prove in the end as absolutist as the One was something the Enlightenment did not prefer to contemplate but that we at the end of a century that has known Auschwitz and the horrors of the gulag can no longer ignore.

Nevertheless, the many have triumphed over the One, and the modern world can be fairly characterized as a place that is comfortable with the displacement of God as the transcendent focus of life.[5] The only question is whether the idea of the many will be able to sustain the culture in whose name it has been called into service. Without God, as Ivan Karamazov knew only too well, anything is permissible, for the problem with the many is its inability to adjudicate questions of truth. If there is no objective meaning or truth undergirding life, if there are only many truths or only "truths for me," then judgments of value and truth are entirely relative matters, expressing the emotions I may feel at any given moment but rooted in nothing deeper. In the world of the many, one opinion is as good as another, and before long we lose confidence in the power of argument to persuade. We are simply talking past one another. So, in the absence of truth, matters are decided simply by "the will to power."[6] Allan Bloom has shown how the pluralism of the many has led to a pluralism of indifference, a "cult of openness" that, paradoxically, has led to the "closing of the American mind":

> Openness used to be the virtue that permitted us to seek the good by using reason. It now means accepting everything and denying reason's power. The unrestrained and thoughtless pursuit of openness, without recognizing the inherent political, social, or cultural problem of openness as the goal of nature, has rendered openness meaningless. . . . Openness to closedness is what we teach.[7]

As a result, the many, often in the name of "openness" or "cultural equality," end up condoning new forms of racism, or censorship, or political tyranny. Indeed, the many, giving rise to a diversity of voices and a variety of points of view, tend to homogenize everything into a pluralism of indifference, in which contending for the truth is itself seen as pointless or as merely disguising the pursuit of power. Thus, the revolt of the many against the One, a revolt that began in an effort to defend those who dared to seek the truth even in the face of ecclesiastical or political intervention, has come to mean doubting whether there is any truth at all. Indeed, the only thing that does not seem to be doubted is the futility of those whose work continues to make claims for the truth.

Colin Gunton has suggested that at bottom this whole debate is really about God and that it is the Christian doctrine of the triune God that enables us to get past the absolutist tyrannies of the One and the homogenizing tendencies of the many, to a life that is characterized by true plurality, rich diversity, and harmony in life together.[8] The Christian doctrine of the Trinity has held that God is three persons in one being, not a blank "Spirit" as the catechism suggests, but a "being in communion," a being whose life is a sharing. But again this sharing is not some homogenized sameness, for the life of Father, Son, and Holy Spirit is characterized by the particularity of each person. There exists a kind of otherness in God, and so it is no accident that we are persons who are different from each other, uniquely and gloriously ourselves. Particularity of time and place and relation, so important in the freedom and development of persons, far from being alien to the triune God, is rooted in the life of Father, Son, and Holy Spirit. Because the world was created by this triune God, who in his Word assumed our own creatureliness, the temporal and limited particularities that constitute our lives are not things to be despised or overcome but to be received as good gifts.

But the triune God is not merely a life of shared particularities. The three persons dwell in unity, held together by the Son in whom all things are held together, "things in heaven and things on earth" (Eph. 1:10). The Greek word for this mutual indwelling or holding together is *perichoresis*, which literally means "dancing around." It is not a bad word to describe the Trinitarian life. If you have seen a country dance, you will understand the aptness of the term. At such a dance the participants, while uniquely themselves, dance in harmony not only with the music but with each other, not being absorbed into each other's roles but playing off of them and coming together in an even deeper and happier unity. Such is God's life, a koinonia or communion, neither a collectivity nor an individual thing but a mutual indwelling, a being in communion.

If human beings are creatures made in the image of this God, then surely we are made for communion with God and each other. Or to put it another way, we become *inhuman* when we forsake this relatedness in the name of a more authoritarian "One" or an indifferent "many." Both subvert our humanity and trivialize our lives.

The human community discovers its true humanity as it is drawn into the life of this Trinitarian dance, a life that celebrates the communion that is ours with God and each other in Jesus Christ. The New Testament name for this life together is "church," whose reason for being is to teach us to dance. Like the triune God whose life the church celebrates, the church can only be understood in terms of its own being in communion, indeed, of its being a body whose members find their lives only in relation to each other.

For Paul, whose language this is, the church is not so much a solution to a problem as it is a sign of hope for all humanity, indeed, a sign of that future redemption awaiting all creation. For a humanity that is always torn between the demands of the One and the contempt of the many, the church's life together in the body of Christ offers the hope of overcoming the fragmentation and loneliness so characteristic of these alternatives. This hope is rooted in the faith that Jesus' story is not just a nice story or an interesting one but is itself the truth about God and this world. In Christ we discover that we are not made for ourselves or to lord it over others, but rather that we are made to dance; we are made for communion. The church becomes, then, a provisional demonstration of this truth, a life together that reflects God's own being in communion with us in Jesus Christ. It is this triune God who alone is willing to risk the folly of teaching us to dance, and so to undermine the grimness of a world bent on saving itself. Yet just so are we incorporated into the body of the Son, becoming the many members held together by his life. In him, we hear the music and proclaim the gospel by dancing. To be caught up in this dance is to discover the joy of true dancing, when we are no longer conscious of ourselves as poor or professional dancers but find ourselves, instead, in the music of the dance itself, "lost in wonder, love, and praise." Then even our groans become signs of hope and "the sufferings of this present time are not worth comparing with the glory about to be revealed to us" (Rom. 8:18).

To tell the truth by dancing may seem a ridiculous way of proclaiming the gospel, but it has the advantage of indicating something of the risk involved. Very few of us can claim to be a Fred Astaire or Ginger Rogers. Even fewer of us resemble Mother Teresa or Martin Luther King Jr. When we try to dance, we run the risk of falling down and exposing our clumsiness. Of course, we do this all the time. The church is a lousy dancer. We long for a less risky way of telling the truth. We are embarrassed by the groans we hear. But the music carries us so that even when we fall, even when we groan, we are lifted beyond ourselves into rhythms and steps where the music begins to master us and we begin to dare to think that we are dancing after all. Otherwise, of course, if we had to be proficient dancers or create the music ourselves, the whole business would be impossible. That it is not is because once, "on the third day, he rose again from the dead." Snoopy is right: "To dance is to live." And there is no telling of this dance that does not involve us in that dancing, that does not invite us to risk making fools of ourselves for Jesus' sake, trusting in him whose life is the music.

Telling such a happy truth is the subject of the next chapter, but already we can hear the music and begin to trace the steps of the dance itself.

5

Telling the Truth as an Act of Faith

*H*ow do we tell the truth? It is easy for us to think that telling the truth is primarily a moral or perhaps a legal issue. Telling the truth is what a witness is sworn to do in a trial, or what we are to do when speaking to each other. It requires of us not only powers of observation but, more particularly, a willingness to state what has happened. "Johnny, did you take a cookie out of the jar?" And Johnny has to face the issue of telling the truth.

Though this may seem a trivial example, the issue of the truth is not. Johnny has to know certain information, and more than that, Johnny has to provide that information even if it means identifying himself as the culprit. In other words, Johnny has to take responsibility for telling the truth. Sometimes that can be very hard, especially if Johnny took the cookie and lives in a home where he is held accountable for his decisions. Suppose, however, that he does not take responsibility. Suppose telling the truth is a matter of some indifference in Johnny's home and is an act that can be engaged in without consulting any larger moral or religious tradition. Then "telling the truth" simply is a matter of saying whatever Johnny feels like saying at the time. Everything depends upon who Johnny thinks he is and what he thinks his life is about. It is the truth that has been told *to* Johnny that matters, the truth that has shaped him, that precedes and enables any other telling of the truth in which he might engage. That is more than a moral or legal matter. That is a question that has to do with faith in God. So how do we tell that truth?

Christian faith has always believed that the truth about human beings is that we are creatures who are made for communion. Augustine in the early fifth century prayed, "O Lord, thou hast made us for thyself and our hearts are restless until they rest in thee." Our hearts are restless, he suggested, because we are made for a particular kind of truth; we are made for communion with God. We long for completion, to understand fully even as we have been fully understood. Augustine thought that our restlessness, which we try to satisfy with money or power or sexual conquests, can only really be satisfied with the truth of the beatific vision, a truth reserved for the next world. Our temporal world is always characterized, he thought, by something short of that truth, an incompleteness and want. Indeed, he was right in his assumption that all our relationships, no matter how intimate or satisfying, are never entirely free from manipulation or fear or issues of power. But the question becomes whether the truth we are after is only an unattainable ideal or something else, a communion that we can taste and see, however dimly, in this life.

As we have noted, the Christian faith has always confessed that true communion is the reality constituted by the life of the triune God. As Christians, we believe that there was a life lived in human history that exhibited a relationship of steadfast love and utter obedience to the one Jesus called "Abba," a relationship sustained in turn by the steadfast love and utter faithfulness of that Father; and that those who believe this Jesus and seek to follow him have been enabled through the presence of the Spirit to participate in the communion of this love, to dance, by the grace of the Lord Jesus Christ, in the triune life of God.[1] Here is the truth we believe to be incarnate in Jesus Christ, the truth that "unites all things in him," things private and things public, things that are called facts and things that are called values, things that we know and things we believe, things in this life and things in the life to come. This is the truth that is sovereign over all of life, the truth that shapes us and keeps us from falling into our own subjectivity on the one hand, or our idols of certitude on the other. This is the truth that nails heaven and earth together. We participate in this truth. In John's Gospel, Jesus prays, "The glory that you have given me I have given them, so that they may be one, as we are one, I in them and you in me" (John 17:22). Here, in the communion that exists between the Father and the Son, the church is drawn by the power of the Spirit, and is given, in Christ's humanity, a place within the circle of God's life. It is out of that triune life that the church bears witness to the world, digesting through word and sacrament the food that builds sinews and muscles, vocal chords and hearts to embrace this world and speak to it gospel words of faith and hope and love. So here is where we start: We begin telling the truth in the place where we have heard the truth, the starting point, not only for Johnny but for us all.

That is why the way we think about God and the way we tell the truth stands or falls with what we confess in the dogmas of the Incarnation and Trinity.[2] Reality is either like the reality we encounter in the Word made flesh, or it is not. The history of the world is either headed toward the goal laid out in Jesus Christ, or it is not. Either this reality informs all the decisions we are called upon to make, or we can safely create our own truths, either retreating into some subjective reality centered within ourselves or resigning ourselves to live in a cold, dark universe that has no meaning at all.

Lest such a stark contrast seem too dramatic, one might attend to some of the other possible starting points being proposed today. Peter Singer, who occupies a distinguished chair of ethics at Princeton University, has received some notoriety recently for proposing that there should be a twenty-eight-day trial period after the birth of a child during which time, should it be defective or unwanted, it might be legally killed: "Since neither a newborn infant nor a fish is a person, the wrongness of killing such beings is not as great as the wrongness of killing a person."[3] What matters is that they not suffer: "We do both infants and fish a wrong if we cause them pain or allow them to suffer, unless to do so is the only way of preventing greater suffering."[4] Singer happily confesses that he has rejected the Judeo-Christian starting point that we are made for communion with God, a starting point that he thinks represents a crumbling ethic in need of replacement by something more nuanced for our more complex age.

One might be tempted to dismiss Singer's views as simply those of a professor making a proposal for further study to his colleagues in the academy. To be sure, there is no need to demonize him. But his views do serve to illustrate the point Lesslie Newbigin makes when he says, "The way we understand human life depends on what conception we have of the human story."[5] If our conception of the human story is that we are here to fulfill ourselves, then what is really wrong with infanticide? Alasdair MacIntyre has suggested that contemporary life has been made almost schizophrenic in its struggle to answer such a question because we are infected still with a great wound the Enlightenment inflicted on the way we think about telling the truth. In order to secure what was thought to be a sound basis of knowledge, the Enlightenment split the world into the realm of facts and the realm of values. Facts are a matter of public knowledge: the battle of Gettysburg, the formula for the circumference of a circle, the distance to the moon. About these we are not pluralistic, that is, we do not generally regard these facts as matters of private opinion. Values, on the other hand, are beliefs, personal decisions that are entirely subjective. About values we agree to be pluralistic, for here questions of truth are not involved, we think, but only of perception. However, as Newbigin points out, a hundred years ago, Scottish school children learned as a fact that "Man's chief end is to glorify God and enjoy him forever." Today such a datum is not a fact but merely a belief, what John Locke would have called "a persuasion of our own minds, short of knowledge."[6]

But what happens to a society or a culture in which this split is so thoroughgoing that we no longer are able to say what human life is for? If we cannot tell Johnny why he was made or what his life is for, then what basis do we have for holding him accountable? In other words, if we no longer believe it is true that human beings are made for God, if we regard such affirmations as a private matter, then what happens when the choices we make are informed by nothing other than our own desires for self-realization? Peter Singer's proposals are one answer. Bigger and stronger human beings can choose, with impunity, whether or not to do away with weaker and more vulnerable human beings. And not only that, but those who are opposed to such proposals will not be able to give a coherent account of their opposition on the basis of this split. Newbigin himself draws out the implications of this question:

> Facts are what we have to reckon with whether we like them or not. Values are what we choose because we want them—either for ourselves or for someone else. Middle-class parents want values to be taught to children in schools because life will be more pleasant if these values are adhered to. But they do not ask whether these values have any relation to the "facts" as taught in school. They do not ask whether it is possible to believe that concern for minorities, for the poor, for the disabled is important if the fact is that human life is the result of the success of the strong in eliminating the weak. If it is a "fact" that human life is the accidental result of ruthless suppression of the weak by the strong, and it is not a fact that "Man's chief end is to glorify God and enjoy him forever," then "values" have no factual basis. They can only be the expression of what some people choose, and—inevitably—it will be the strong who prevail. The language of "values" is simply the will to power wrapped up in cotton wool. And we cannot use the language of right and wrong because it has no basis in the "facts" as we understand them.[7]

The split between facts and values makes it impossible to tell the truth. Facts have no moral language; they are simply the result of cause and effect. And values have no factual basis; they are simply the expression of what we choose at a given time. The effort to read some universal moral claim out of facts always runs aground on the realization that such a claim is itself a residue of faith. But faith, this split has decreed, is a private affair and can yield only a subjective truth, a "truth for me." The result, as Alasdair MacIntyre has shown, is that moral reflection has broken loose from any tradition that cultivates *knowledge* of the truth or embodies the virtues that include telling the truth, such that we are simply thrown back on ourselves, unable to share anymore in a truth to tell.[8] Moreover, facts inevitably appear in this view to be quite purposeless things. Our knowledge of them has no ultimate end or purpose, just as our values have no roots in some deeper tradition. The result is a kind of hopeless society, a culture that lacks any sense of a worthwhile future. Indeed, that is why hopelessness is the pervasive undercurrent of so much of contemporary life. A culture that takes this split between facts and values as axiomatic cannot help but manifest its hopelessness in increasingly desperate acts of violence, in the suicide of young and old, in sexual promiscuity that promises to relieve the numbness but only increases the despair.

A culture that is divided at its very heart cannot stand. To overcome such a division, a new starting point will have to be found, a starting point that will not be afraid of asking the question of purpose. The split between facts and values was originally proposed to exclude this question because, it was argued, whenever the question of purpose enters the discussion, our knowledge inevitably ties itself up in knots. It is enough to know the cause and effect of things. But is it? Is it enough to know how human beings are conceived, how they thrive, even how they die, and not know what they are for? Why not wait until a baby is twenty-eight days old before deciding whether or not it is human enough to keep? What is so wrong with that? Or with what happened to mentally defective children during the Third Reich? If my values are merely my own creation and not rooted in the fact of Jesus Christ, then what would really be so wrong in throwing in my lot with the Nazis or assisting in their extermination of these children? Are such questions answerable apart from the deeper question of the nature and the purpose of human life? But what if we refuse to answer *that* question? But that is *the* question and that is why the fissure between the world of facts and the world of values cannot be healed unless the matter of purpose is reopened and dealt with.

How shall we do that? Such a question is not merely an idle one or one that proposes to take the commanding heights of our culture by storm. Rather, such a question simply asks what Dietrich Bonhoeffer asked in his day, namely, "What is the meaning of Jesus Christ for us today?" The heart of the gospel is the claim that in Jesus Christ the Word became flesh. He is the purpose in whom all things unite (Eph. 1:10). Nothing, Paul reminds us, is able to separate us from his love. Nothing. So Christians are constitutionally unable to take any split between facts and values as axiomatic, as the last word about human life, about our knowing and believing. Such a split here will mean, sooner or later, a split between the strong and the weak, between Jew and Greek, slave and free, male and female. But these are, we are told, all one in Christ (Gal. 3:28). Overcoming this deep wound, then, is exactly what the gospel attests that Jesus Christ does, and the task of the church is nothing less than to convert such a culture to the healing unity that is ours in him. That is why learning to tell and speak the truth is finally a missionary activity, undertaken by the church both for Johnny's sake and for the world's.

We can begin to see something of what is involved in this task by looking at two slogans or mottoes that, Newbigin suggests, have attempted to describe the work of discerning and telling the truth, both for the believer and for the scientist. The first is from Descartes, who thought telling the truth could only be guaranteed when it has passed through the fires of my own skepticism and achieved certainty through my own reflection: "I think, therefore I am." (*Cogito ergo sum*). Knowledge, thought Descartes, has to be certain. This desire for certainty represented a longing to have things settled, to possess a degree of certitude that would make knowledge impregnable, that would deliver us into a realm of such security that we would no longer have to depend upon another to justify or defend us. Our words, our calculations would be enough in themselves and would be timelessly and universally true. Descartes was after a knowledge that would be without risk, a knowledge that would not embarrass us but would be complete in itself. Such knowledge, he thought, could be found not through anything so "uncertain" as the faithfulness of God but in the certainty of our own minds.[9]

This desire for a "riskless" truth, a truth that requires neither a personal commitment nor the limping that characterizes those who wait upon the faithfulness of God, is very attractive to us. It holds out the promise of settling things without requiring our own involvement. In its religious form, it comes to us in a kind of biblical fundamentalism that promises a reading of the scripture that will free the believer of any error and grant a certainty that requires neither faithful discernment nor awkward limping. All that is needed are proof texts that will silence doubters. In its scientific form, this notion of "riskless" truth comes to us as a kind of a scientism, a reading of the "facts" of nature that are simply to be accepted and that call for no personal decision.[10] Neither of these "riskless" forms of the truth will ever embarrass us, and in the end both will allow us to use them to shore up our own positions. But strangely, neither of these forms describe the way scientists and believers have actually gone about the task of apprehending and speaking the truth. To examine that, we must look at the other motto that Newbigin proposes.

"*Credo ut intelligam*" ("I believe that I may understand").[11] So prayed Augustine some 1500 years ago. This starting point assumes that knowing the truth is a risky business. To know something, we must first assume that it is knowable, that it can be probed, explored, discerned. A scientist brings an enormous amount of personal commitment to the task before her. She might be wrong, she might possess the wrong tools, she might have to grope her way along, almost as if she were limping. But she believes that what she is seeking to know is intelligible, not simply a product of her own imagination. There is a "there" out there. And because of her own commitment to that reality, she is willing to submit herself to the discipline and life of a larger tradition that shares with her this quest and whose ways she must master in order to probe more deeply. Like a craftsman learning to paint or plumb, the scientist is part of a community of learning, the heir of a long tradition of craftsmanship and learning as well as a practitioner of the craft, even an explorer seeking to carry the tradition farther. Just so, the scientist will publish her findings, holding herself accountable to the tradition that has helped shape her questions and equipped her for the work of understanding. She may, at times, find herself at odds with that tradition or even seek to persuade the scientific community that it has overlooked something important or turned down the wrong path. But even then, she will incur that risk and invite comment not to vindicate a private opinion but in the hope that her views will strengthen the tradition and put the universal acceptance of its truth on even firmer ground. She believes in order to understand.

Christians too belong to a tradition, a community of interpretation and practice. We submit ourselves to the learning of the larger community, finding models for our faith in the words and lives of saintly people who teach us by embodying for us the grace of our Lord Jesus Christ. In this tradition, we also believe in order to understand. Here too we may be wrong. Limping is the characteristic way Christians walk in seeking to follow Jesus Christ, for in following him, every Christian runs the risk of being just like the disciples in the gospel story, of misunderstanding what Jesus is telling us, of failing him at crucial times, of needing his presence constantly to find the way. There is no formula that will secure us from such embarrassment. Indeed, knowledge of the truth does not come without such humbling risks. It is always possible for us to speak the truth but not in love, such that the truth we honor becomes a kind of deadly weapon. It is also possible for us to love untruthfully so that the love we share becomes a cheap lie, complicit in the evils we would otherwise deplore. Moreover, the truth of the faith is not easily assimilated to the many ways we seek to protect ourselves from falsehood or embarrassment in other areas of life. A seminary full of credentialed Ph.D.'s, for example, proves distressingly as sinful a place as the local congregation. The training in this tradition humbles all, even as it invites all to participate in the life and purpose narrated in Jesus Christ.

Similarly, our worship and our service require enormous personal commitment. The God of Jesus Christ is the God whose life is one of utter faithfulness, the God who calls forth a response of faith. To know this God is not simply to have information, however reliable, about him. Rather, to know this God is to trust in him, to receive our lives from his own hands. This commitment is neither a pious wish nor a "belief in believing." Rather, to be open to God here means to confess faith in him even from the ash heap of our broken dreams, trusting in God's final vindication in the face of suffering and loss. Moreover, the test of this risking such a commitment is not the sincerity of our feelings about the truth we seek, but our willingness to "publish" what we know, that is, to embody this tradition in our own lives, to hold ourselves accountable to it for our own findings, to carry it forward through the establishment of communities of faith.[12]

How do Christians "publish" their findings? How do we convert a culture split between its facts and its values, helping it to see its deeper unity in God's purpose for this world? We do not do so by seeking to explain to that culture how useful Christ might be in furthering its goals. There is no goal more ultimate than Jesus Christ. But neither do we do so by merely preaching "at" the culture. Rather, we "publish" the good news of what God has done in Jesus Christ, inviting the world to believe in him by celebrating this good news in that life together he has made possible. We establish churches. We find our life in the life of a worshiping community. We join with others in Christ's mission to this world. To be sure, we often feel our way along and even stumble. Moreover, we learn as much about the gospel from those whom we seek to reach as they will ever learn from us. Inevitably, however, we will find ourselves believing in order to understand. As Newbigin concludes:

> To be willing so to publish them [our beliefs] is the test of our real belief. In this sense missions are the test of our faith. We believe that the truth about the human story has been disclosed in the events which form the substance of the gospel. We believe, therefore, that these events are the real clue to the story of every person, for every human life is part of the whole human story and cannot be understood apart from that story. It follows that the test of our real belief is our readiness to share it with all people.[13]

Perhaps it sounds too simplistic to say that the splits that threaten to divide our culture can be overcome by anything so pedestrian as the church's life and witness. It would be too simplistic if all that were involved were some intellectual muddle. But the problem is not confusion but hopelessness, not complexity but a deep wound. The split between facts and values matters not because it is an intellectual conundrum but because it is evidence of a deep hopelessness that is eating away at our culture's life. The resulting moral relativism that no longer has a passion for the truth but contents itself with what is "true for me" is itself a sign of hopelessness, a last despairing effort struggling not to have to face the relentless fact of Jesus Christ, whose life alone gives value to all of life. To want to evade this claim "is the mark of a tragic loss of nerve in our contemporary culture. It is a preliminary symptom of death."[14] The question is not how to solve this puzzle but how to heal this wound, how to overcome this despair, how to recover confidence in the truth. And the church has no other antidote to offer than him who is the way, the truth, and the life, the one who, after all, was raised from the dead and in whose company confused and despairing disciples have always been surprised by hope.

How is the wound healed? Hope enters the bloodstream of a culture through communities of hope, through congregations, through small platoons of faithful people who live out of the truth of the Word made flesh. Easter's truth creates hope out of despair, just as the life of the risen Lord creates community out of divided hearts. In him there is a narrative that runs counter to the stories our culture tells us that might makes right. In him there is a purpose that "scatters the proud in the imagination of their hearts," even as it puts "down the mighty from their thrones"(Luke 1:52). In him there is a joy that delights in what is good, that "exalts those of low degree," even as it "fills the hungry with good things" (Luke 1:53). The church has nothing else to offer this world but this story, this life we know in Jesus Christ. This is the life that alone creates a worthwhile future. What else do we have to offer the world? Our expertise? Our philosophy? Our superior management skills? None of these things will ever heal the splits that divide our hearts and our culture. Only Jesus Christ can heal such splits, for only on his cross has the true purpose of this world been revealed in God's decision to nail heaven and earth together in him. At the heart of the church's efforts to "publish" its findings then is simply the desire to be with Jesus. And where is he?

> Where he is is on that frontier which runs between the kingdom of God and the usurped power of the evil one. When Jesus sent out his disciples on his mission, he showed them his hands and his side. They will share in his mission as they share in his passion, as they follow him in challenging and unmasking the powers of evil. There is no other way to be with him. At the heart of mission is simply the desire to be with him and to give him the service of our lives. At the heart of mission is thanksgiving and

praise. We distort matters when we can justify ourselves by our works. . . . The church's mission began as the radioactive fallout from an explosion of joy. When it is true to its nature, it is so to the end. Mission is an acted out doxology. That is its deepest secret. Its purpose is that God may be glorified.[15]

One of the great temptations of the Christian faith is to want a faith whose affirmations will cost us nothing. The truth is that knowing and speaking the truth has always been a risky business. It certainly was for Jesus. It is a measure of how comfortable we have grown as Christians that we have to be reminded that the one whom we worship died, after all, on a cross. It is salutary to reflect why Jesus was killed. After all, if I'm okay and you're okay, then why is he up on that cross? If the truth is only a "truth for me," then Jesus really need not have gone to so much trouble. And if the truth is not a matter that costs us our very lives, then why bother telling it?

Along with our desire to reduce the faith to a set of costless affirmations is a yearning for a truth that will not give offense. In part, such an impulse rightly reminds us that the Christian faith is not advanced when it seeks to be deliberately offensive, when it speaks the truth without love or on the basis of some less worthy motivation. Yet, if the heart of the Christian faith is the cross, then it is impossible to proclaim this gospel without giving offense. Indeed, unless and until we are offended by its claims, we have not heard them aright. Those who rejected Jesus in the gospel narratives were often those who understood him best, who understood that if his truth were in fact sovereign, their little kingdoms, their understanding of themselves, their efforts to sustain a separate truth would be finished. Rejection is not always a sign of being misunderstood. Sometimes it is a sign of being understood very well indeed.

What is hard is living with rejection, even learning to love those who reject us. We would rather live with a truth that did not make such demands upon us, that would allow us to make costless affirmations and enjoy a harmless neutrality. That way being a Christian would be more manageable and would not require the miracle of having to love our enemies. But Jesus does not seem to be afraid of relying on such a miracle anymore than of being rejected. What he resists is the effort to live by something less costly than the faithfulness of God's grace. His call to us is to love our world enough to risk telling it the truth, to love our children enough to teach them the ways of this faithful God, to love our culture enough to embrace it for Jesus' sake.

There is nothing neutral about such an embrace. Indeed, unless we believe that Jesus Christ is the way God has embraced this world, there is no reason for us to bother anyone else with this story. But if it is the truth that God does embrace us in Jesus Christ, then to embrace this world will always be a costly matter, and will require our reaching out to those who believe differently than we do, who do not believe anything at all, and who may well be offended by our faith.

6

Other Voices, Other Claims:
The Gospel and Other Religions

*R*ecently I was in Houston and decided to venture into the part of town where I had grown up. I had not driven down our street in more than thirty years, and I wondered what our house would look like and how well the neighborhood was holding up. We were the first family to live in our house and one of the first families to move into our addition. It was the 1950s, and Houston was well into the postwar housing boom. Our addition was planted on a piece of Gulf prairie, backing up to Brays Bayou, and full of wildflowers, vacant lots, and new schools and shopping centers. Like so many other families at that time, we found ourselves in a young, raw, almost instant neighborhood, with lots of kids and young parents just starting out.

We were mostly Protestant, as I recall. There were a few Catholics, even fewer Jews, and no Muslims or Buddhists at all. A Mormon church was just getting started and we thought them exotic enough. Mostly we were Baptists or Methodists or Presbyterians or Lutherans or Episcopalians. There were some members of the Church of Christ and a small but rapidly growing nondenominational church that was rumored to speak in tongues. We were entirely white, though on the other side of the bayou there were some Hispanic families and in other parts of town large numbers of what we called then Negroes.

As I approached my old neighborhood, I noticed that many of the street signs were in Chinese. Some of the stores near the church where we worshiped advertised in what appeared to be Korean. On the site of what used to be a grocery store was now a mosque, and the next addition over housed a Hindu temple. The elementary school that I attended was now filled with a variety of races: Asians, African Americans, Hispanics. I had heard that there were fifteen different language groups represented at that school.

Few would contest that we live in a pluralistic world. As Terry Muck has pointed out, the presence of large numbers of committed believers in what appears to us to be "alien gods" is now commonplace in most of our large cities.[1] For people like myself, who grew up in a much more homogenous (and indeed, a much more Protestant) world, these other voices appear to be a new and not entirely unwelcome presence that we must reckon with. We proclaim the gospel as true in a world full of rival claims, differing points of view, other notions of salvation, alternative understandings of God. Yet if this understanding is new, it is so only because it is new to us who have been sheltered from the world's variety by factors of history and geography, as well as by our own assimilation to a culture that has not taken religious differences seriously.

However, the presence of rival claims and "strange" gods is not new. It certainly would not have surprised Israel or the early church. Israel's peculiar calling as God's people worked itself out against the background of the gods of other nations, of Baal and Moloch, of the gods of Egypt and Canaan and Babylon. Indeed, Israel was awash in a sea of competing religious claims, as was the early church. According to Matthew, Jesus' birth was of interest to "wise men from the East"(Matt. 2:1). In his own ministry, Jesus engaged the Samaritan woman concerning the question of "true worship" and had substantial theological exchanges, not only with Pharisees like Nicodemus (John 3), but also with folk as varied as the Syrophoenician woman (Mark 7:26) and a Roman centurion (Matt. 8:5–13). At one point, Paul and Barnabas were welcomed by the inhabitants of Lystra as the Greek gods, Zeus and Hermes. Paul preached in Athens not only to the Epicurean and Stoic philosophers but also to a city he called "very religious," a city full of so many objects of worship that it even had an altar to an "unknown god" (Acts 17:23). The gospel was originally proclaimed and took root in a pluralistic world, a world where rival religious and philosophical claims permeated the culture and were much more established than the Christian faith. Early Christian writers such as Justin Martyr and the author of the *Letter to Diognetus* sought explicitly to interpret the Christian faith to this culture, sometimes drawing upon ideas and terms which that culture had already developed. Other theologians such as Irenaeus and Athanasius sought to distinguish the Christian faith from what they regarded as cultural counterfeits. Yet, whether in pagan Rome or in the dark forests of Europe, whether under an Islamic caliphate or amidst a Hellenistic culture, Christians in the first millennium of the church's life were keenly aware of alternative claims to the gospel and struggled to meet the challenges of living faithfully in such a milieu.

It is helpful to remember this because we are sometimes told that pluralism represents a crisis in the life of the church. But in fact, the church was born into a world of pluralistic claims, and if there is a crisis, it has less to do with the church's faith than it does with our culture's notion of pluralism. It is one thing to note that there are differences in what people believe. That is a kind of "descriptive pluralism" about which there is no debate. The church was born into such a world and lives in such a world today. But it is quite another thing to say that such differences preclude any claims to the truth. Such an assertion represents a kind of "prescriptive pluralism,"[2] a judgment that possesses information about religion in general that allows it to exclude particular claims to the truth as divisive or imperialistic. Prescriptive pluralism rests on a prior assumption that all religions are essentially alike, each one describing a particular experience from a single vantage point. Obviously, given such an understanding, no one religion can claim to possess anything more than a relative point of view. Accordingly, claims to the truth are simply not to be pressed, for such claims will result in unresolved and unresolvable conflict. Indeed, that has been the attractiveness of prescriptive pluralism. It has held out the promise of cultivating tolerance among the various religions, a tolerance of religions enforced by the culture's agreement that certain questions not be raised. It is this cultural settlement, however, that is in crisis today, for it is unable to give an account of its own privileged position, much less its reasons for thinking that all religions are species of the same genus.

At first glance, the kind of pluralism that forbids particular claims to truth as out of bounds appears modest. After all, the truth is greater than our thoughts can grasp and is greater than what one person or one tradition can embody. Moreover, all of us have had encounters with "sole possessors of the truth" that have left us unimpressed, or perhaps even longing for something less than the "truth." As Richard John Neuhaus has reminded us, whatever else the will of God is, it is surely the will of God that we not kill each other fighting over what is the will of God.

On the other hand, the fact that the truth is greater than our thoughts can sometimes be used as an argument against the affirmation of any truth. One of the most basic claims of the Enlightenment was that because God remains impenetrably hidden from us, we cannot really be said to know God. We are finally thrown back either on our sense of morality or subjective experience of the infinite and so discover from within ourselves a sense of our dependence on the divine. This sense, however, tells us nothing about God, only about our experience of God. Our situation is like the parable of the blind man and the elephant, each of us describing what God is like "for me."

Lesslie Newbigin points out that that parable has often been misinterpreted and its main point overlooked:

> The story is told from the point of view of the king and of his courtiers, who are not blind but can see that the blind men are unable to grasp the full reality of the elephant and are only able to get hold of part of the truth. The story is constantly told in order to neutralize the affirmation of the great religions, to suggest that they learn humility and recognize that none of them can have more than one aspect of the truth. But, of course, the real point of the story is exactly the opposite. If the king were also blind there would be no story. The story is told by the king, and it is the immensely arrogant claim of one who sees the full truth which all the religions are only groping after. It embodies the claim to know the full reality which relativizes all the claims of the religions and philosophies.[3]

Newbigin knows that in a culture that thinks it sees better than the pitifully blind folk who are struggling to describe God, any robust statement of faith, any claim to confess the truth about God or God's purpose for humankind will always be unwelcome. It will likely be dismissed as ignorant at best, dogmatic at worst. Yet in interpreting the parable in light of the one in whose benefit it was originally told (i.e., the king), Newbigin points out the arrogance underlying the claim to see all religions from some superior vantage point. The question to be asked, of course, is on what basis does the king see so well? Or to put it another way, on what basis does a prescriptive pluralism have information about religious claims that allows it to see the complete truth while the faithful remain blind?

Are all religions really saying the same thing? From what we can gather by listening to such people of the faith, they have deep reservations about any effort to blur the distinctions between their own particular claims. Buddhist writers, for example, have not welcomed the suggestion that Taoism, Confucianism, and Buddhism are merely different ways of saying the same thing.[4] Similarly, just as the New Testament is clear in stating that Jesus died on the cross, the Qur'an is equally insistent that he did not. Are these differences reconcilable? Are they just different ways of saying the same thing? Alister McGrath focuses on just this question:

> The fundamental importance of this point is totally beyond dispute. It matters decisively whether Jesus Christ died upon the cross, both as history and theology. The historical aspect of the question is crucial: both the New Testament and the Qur'an cannot be right. If one is correct on this historical issue, the other is incorrect. . . . The theological aspects of the matter are also beyond dispute. If Jesus did not die on the cross, an entire series of distinctively and authentically Christian beliefs is called into question. . . . [I]f Jesus Christ did not die on the cross, there is no Christian gospel.[5]

Is there not something patronizing and false in treating all religions as merely different species of the same genus? What sin have we committed when we disagree with each other? Why is it that modern historical consciousness is so fearful of particular claims to the truth? Is there some other agenda being protected here? Is not such a pluralism the product of a particular culture too? How is it able to see better than those whose faith is embodied in a more explicitly religious tradition?

There is a rightful longing for peace and unity among all people. Moreover, the history of religious conflict, whether in the Middle East or India or the Balkans or Northern Ireland, is a sad one indeed and is not one that warrants much faith in the effectiveness of "sweetness and light." Pious expressions of goodwill are simply not enough here. Indeed, that is why the story of the blind men and the elephant was originally told, because the question of how we are to live together peaceably amidst our differences is not an idle question. Convictions of faith are dangerous things, as anyone can tell who reads, for example, the Bible or the newspaper. It has only been possible to think otherwise in a culture that regularly assures us that religious differences do not really matter.

Unfortunately, that has been the basis for much of our talk about tolerance. In the story of the blind men and the elephant, tolerance is recommended as a virtue on the grounds that our blindness requires a forbearing of judgment, even a refusal to judge because each of us sees only part of the picture. Of course, it is the superior point of view of the king that makes this recommendation possible. Nevertheless, the act of tolerating becomes the basis for some measure of life together through a mutually agreed upon withdrawal of claims to the truth.

The problem with this solution is twofold. First of all, by compelling the withdrawal of any claim to the truth, the faith of the believer is turned into a private matter and emptied of any cosmic or political or historical significance. We become our own source of "spirituality," which, of course, is what has trivialized our faith so radically today. But secondly, it makes tolerance too easy. If tolerance is merely the forbearing from judgment and is a virtue unrooted in any larger claim to the truth, then there are no criteria for accepting or rejecting another's point of view or action. All is permitted. Since none of us has the whole answer, each of us must forbear judgment. Tolerance then becomes indistinguishable from indifference, a despairing resignation rather than a genuine struggle to live faithfully in the face of ideas or types of behavior with which we disagree.

But what if true tolerance is not some neutral forbearance from judgment that dismisses all alternatives as equally flawed or accepts them as equally agreeable but is, rather, the fruit of judgment? That is, what if tolerance is a virtue that is only possible in the company of other virtues and is itself sustained by an even deeper conviction of faith?[6] Is not true tolerance only able to bear with alien expressions of belief or objectionable courses of action because it is itself deeply rooted in a narrative of faith that it believes to be true? And is it not this narrative of faith that sustains the willingness to bear even the alien or the objectionable as a witness to its own understanding of the gospel?

Tolerance is an act of faith, an act that has to consult the heart of faith's own narrative in order to bear its particular witness to the truth. John Budziszewski offers this example:

> In colonial America, Nathaniel Ward preached the use of force against heresy for the sake of saving souls, intolerance for God's sake. . . . But Roger Williams asked *What if souls cannot be saved in that way?* And *What if persecution is not what God wants?* He argued that the sword breeds a nation of hypocrites, that the loving God does not require blood, and that scripture teaches other means of persuasion. In preaching tolerance he loved God not worse than Nathaniel Ward, but better.[7]

That is why true tolerance never forbears to judge but is always the fruit of judgment, a judgment that begins by searching the story that has shaped our deepest convictions. To be sure, if we have forgotten that story or no longer think that tolerance is a matter of faith, then tolerance will soon enough turn into indifference and become as arrogant or imperialistic as the very claims it seeks to mediate. Worse, it will accept the wrong things, becoming complicit in the schemes of the powerful over against the weak, "tolerating" the abuses of a totalitarian state while ignoring the plight of a despised minority. To judge well, tolerance must always have a memory of its own story and be able to consult its own faith.

Moreover, true tolerance is a virtue that never stands alone but only in the company of other virtues that a life of faith cultivates, virtues that Paul describes as "the fruit of the Spirit" (i.e., love, joy, peace, patience, kindness, goodness, faithfulness, gentleness, self-control). It is these that enable tolerance to endure certain evils for the sake of keeping faith with the larger good that God has revealed in the cross of Jesus Christ. There, Christians affirm, good really did triumph over evil, but precisely not by the use of force to eradicate it from the earth but by bearing evil, and bearing it away, "enduring the cross, disregarding its shame" (Heb. 12:2), confident that God's truth is vindicated even in weakness just as it will one day be revealed in glory. The cross is the real basis for true tolerance, and the cross compels us to take seriously not only the life but also the convictions of our neighbors.

How then shall we live together among a diversity of traditions? What should be our stance in proclaiming the faith in such a world?

If the cross of Jesus Christ is in fact the central clue we have in understanding God's love for this world, then perhaps we ought to begin there in trying to address our near and distant neighbors. The following suggestions might serve as a place to start.

First, the cross of Jesus Christ tells us that faith is not a trivial matter. Jesus was not killed in a private dispute. Faith, therefore, cannot in the end be reduced to politics or ethics or consumer choice; faith goes to the heart of what we think is important about life. Therefore, Christians have no alternative but to take seriously the faith of other people, no matter what that faith is. Whatever they believe, however strange or odd we might find it, is not something that Christians can simply dismiss out of hand. The modern world is never more captive to its own illusions than when it dismisses faith as merely a private or trivial matter. Religion, unfortunately, often testifies to its central significance in our own day with its pervasive presence in human conflict. People do not fight over things that do not matter to them. We do them no service by belittling what they believe. If we are to engage people of other faiths in conversation, then such a conversation must grow out of a deep respect for their beliefs, a respect that begins by listening to them and taking seriously what they believe.

Second, the cross of Jesus Christ teaches us to expect his grace to be at work in the world, even in lives that do not yet confess him as Lord. The psalmist asks, "Where can I go from your spirit? Or where can I flee from your presence? If I ascend to heaven, you are there; if I make my bed in Sheol, you are there" (Ps. 139:7–8).

Peter discovers that the Holy Spirit has been at work in Cornelius long before Peter arrives on the scene. The Ethiopian eunuch asks Philip if the words from Isaiah 53 refer to the prophet Isaiah or to someone else. The New Testament expectation is that Jesus is Lord and it is this reality that precedes all our questions and answers, becoming itself the context for our engagement with others. In fact, something like that was Jonah's great fear, namely, that God would be at work in the hearts of the Ninevites before Jonah's prophecy of doom could take place, which, of course, is what happened. When we proclaim the gospel of Jesus Christ, or when we engage people of other faith in conversation, we can only do so in the confidence that Jesus Christ has already been at work in their lives and in their hearts. What else does our baptism tell us but that Jesus has claimed us in exactly this way? "We love him because he first loved us." The old hymn says it well: "I sought the Lord and afterward, I knew, he moved my heart to seek him seeking me; 'twas not I that found O Savior true; No, I was found of thee."

Third, the cross is the place where sinners gather. On the one hand, this is an appropriate reminder that all our words are flawed, even our most ardent and sincere words of faith, and need therefore the grace of our Lord Jesus Christ to help them speak faithfully and aright. But on the other hand, the cross reminds us that even as sinners we belong to a community of Jesus Christ and therefore are right to look for ways to join with others in community, celebrating life together. The Christian, according to Lesslie Newbigin, "will be eager to cooperate with people of all faiths and ideologies in projects which are in line with the Christian's understanding of God's purpose in history."[8] Whatever else the cross means, it surely is not an invitation to forsake the realities of this life for some "spiritual" realm where as individuals we are untouched by the lives of others. God takes our time and place seriously, and just so invites us to love the world he has made. Christians will most effectively engage the world with the truth of the faith when we love the people and the communities in which we find ourselves, joining with others to build community and to celebrate the good things of the culture. To be sure, not all causes, not even all community-building efforts, are ones that Christians can join or endorse. The cross never invites us to forsake this world for a more privileged position but to embrace this world in all its diversity and variety, working to find with others that common ground where we can stand together. We believe that ground has been prepared by the cross of Jesus Christ. Others do not. Yet if we stand with them where and when we can, we testify to our hope that one day we will indeed all stand together.

Fourth, the cross of Jesus Christ is the place where real differences can emerge and so real conversation can take place. Jesus Christ has ever been a stumbling block to believers and nonbelievers alike, which is why we have often hoped that we could engage others in something less scandalous, something like "religion in general." But "religion in general" is harmless and shows little interest in a love that would go to such lengths to seek us out. God's love, however, is relentless in its willingness to embarrass us, and the cross is the great sign of that embarrassment. Here is where real conversation can begin, that is, at the point where God's scandalous love for sinners is brought to incandescence in Jesus Christ. Here we simply point to him as we work and live side by side with others. We point to him not because we despise other religions or think we are in possession of a commodity others do not have. Rather, we point to him for the same reason we tell our children of his gospel. Here is the one gift with which we are entrusted that we cannot hoard, the one talent we cannot bury. Here is the love we cannot escape, the life that we would not be without. We belong to one who has drawn us into a life not of our choosing and has made us a part of a community peopled with folk whom we have not selected. He has entrusted us with this particular story, a story that when lived out necessarily points beyond itself to Jesus Christ. He is the question that questions us, the scandal that embarrasses us, the love that relentlessly pursues us. It is not within our power to convert anyone to this story, but we are called to live it out with exuberance and joy, loving the culture in which we find ourselves, the people who are our neighbors, the strangers who are within our gates. God will do the rest.

Does this mean that all will be saved? What happens to Buddhists or Muslims or Marxists or atheists when they die? Will they go to heaven? What if the substance of their lives is in every way more worthy and honorable than that of many Christians? What will happen to them?

Truly, there are some questions before which we should be modestly silent. Reflecting on the cross should lead us to humility before God's grace rather than to some presumed or garrulous knowledge. In the eleventh chapter of Romans, Paul ends his reflection on this whole matter by lifting up his hands in a doxology, confessing his own ignorance before the mysteries of God's grace: "O the depths of the riches and wisdom and knowledge of God! How unsearchable are his judgments and how inscrutable his ways!" (Rom. 11:33). The truth is, we do not know the answers to these questions and they are not our business to know. This is God's business. But we do not have to know. It is enough for us to trust in Jesus Christ. For only in him is there salvation, for ourselves and for our neighbor. Who will set the limits to his abundant grace? Who indeed? "For God has imprisoned all in disobedience so that he may be merciful to all" (Rom. 11:32).

It is relatively easy for us to think about the Christian faith as having to do with our own salvation or, perhaps, having to do with improving the moral character of the culture in which we live. It is much more difficult, however, for us to believe that the central claim of the gospel is that in Jesus Christ true human unity has been established. Here is the universal claim of the gospel in all its scandalous catholicity. Here all peoples may find their reconciliation; here all the things we take so seriously as "dividing walls of hostility" are broken down. If we do not proclaim that the cross of Jesus Christ is the place where all humanity is reconciled and made one, then we should not be surprised if other claimants arise: the nation-state, the political party, racial ideologies, other demons only too eager to set up house in the body politic or the body of Christ. Indeed, as Newbigin notes,

The Christian gospel has sometimes been made the tool of an imperialism, and of that we have to repent. But at its heart it is the denial of all imperialism, for at its center there is the cross where all imperialisms are humbled and we are invited to find the center of human unity in the One who was made nothing so that all might be one. The very heart of the biblical vision for the unity of humankind is that its center is not an imperial power but the slain Lamb.[9]

The cross reserves its most painful questions for those who would make of it yet another imperialism, and it reserves its most embarrassing rebukes for those who would avoid its path in order to find a less costly way of proclaiming its truth. But even so, the cross makes an undeniably universal claim, a claim that cannot be reduced in scope or made more manageable in practice. This claim is that all humanity finds its rightful place only at the banquet table of the Lamb. There we join with all creation, with myriads of angels, singing, "Worthy is the Lamb that was slaughtered, to receive power and wealth and wisdom and might and honor and glory and blessing!" (Rev. 5:12).

7

Feeling Uncomfortable at Home: The Gospel's Encounter with North American Paganism

Several years ago, I served on a committee charged with examining candidates for the ministry. The chair of our committee was an old pastor approaching retirement who had served the church well in a variety of positions and had been faithful over little and over much. Often he would take the lead in these ordination exams, always asking the same question: "Who is God?" If the candidate recited the catechism's answer—"God is a Spirit, infinite, unchangeable in his being wisdom, holiness, justice, goodness and truth"—that was all right with the old pastor, at least as a place to start. On the other hand, if the candidate wanted to talk about the doctrine of the Trinity or God's self-revelation in Jesus Christ, that would be even better. Most often, the candidate would offer some personal statement of faith, sometimes referring to a moment of illumination or a particularly powerful experience. Still, the chairman would ask the same question of every candidate: "Who is God?"

At one meeting, I think it must have been in the late 1970s or early 1980s, there came a young candidate for ordination who had recently graduated from a divinity school in the East. She was a daughter of a congregation within our own presbytery and hoped to go into pastoral counseling. The examination began as it usually did with our chairman leading off with his question, "Miss Smith, tell me, who is God?"

After a pause, Miss Smith looked at the old pastor and, calling him by his first name, said, "David, God is a rainbow."

Her answer flummoxed our chairman, and for a moment he did not know how to proceed. "What do you mean, God is a rainbow?" he asked. "Well," she replied, "God is a prism of light into ourselves. Some of us see green or red or purple; others see yellow or blue. But God is a rainbow and can be pretty much what we want to see."

So began a long and unhappy examination. I think of that old pastor who thought he had heard it all, a pastor who had spent his life serving the church in congregations and seminaries, stunned to discover after all these years that God was a rainbow.

Yet the answer the young woman gave was utterly sincere. For her, "God" was the name of some deeper knowledge of self, and on this occasion at least, happily identified with the image of a rainbow. When pushed to elaborate on this definition, what emerged was God's plasticity, the various colors, the infinite ways in which God's presence could be discovered within the self. What this might have to do with the narrative of Jesus Christ, or the revelation of God's love on the cross, or the community of memory and hope shaped by that event never became quite clear, as I recall. If God were a rainbow, then it was up to the individual to perceive and benefit from this experience.

Harold Bloom would have understood. He is a distinguished professor of English literature who teaches at Yale University. In 1992, he wrote a book entitled, *The American Religion: The Emergence of the Post-Christian Nation*. Though Bloom's field is literature and though he himself is a Jewish agnostic, his book offers an illuminating interpretation of what religion in North America has become. Early on he sums up his views:

> Unlike most countries, we have no overt national religion, but a partly concealed one has been developing among us for some two centuries now. It is almost purely experiential, and despite its insistences, it is scarcely Christian in any traditional way. A religion of the self burgeons, under many names, and seeks to

know its own inwardness, in isolation. What the American self has found, since about 1800, is its own freedom—from the world, from time, from other selves. But this freedom is a very expensive torso, because of what it is obliged to leave out: society, temporality, the other. What remains, for it, is solitude and the abyss.[1]

Bloom thinks that this American belief in self has taken up residence particularly in Protestant Christianity and threatens to reduce it to something akin to ancient gnosticism, that is, to a knowledge that allows us to escape the limits of "nature, time, history, community, and other selves."[2] In other words, God is a rainbow. Salvation, in this view, is not mediated through Jesus Christ or celebrated in the life that is his body, the church, but comes through a knowledge of self, a knowledge that frees the individual from the limitations of such communities, even from the limitations of time and space. Bloom goes so far as to argue that this gnostic (from the Greek word, *gnosis*, meaning "knowledge") tendency has always been present in American religion and even constitutes its chief characteristic. He even anticipates its final victory as the truly American religion "because it so subtly kills the great enemy of gnosticism—i.e., Christianity."[3]

Bloom, though no friend of the Christian faith, is on to something in understanding Christianity as the enemy of gnosticism. However, even before Bloom wrote his book, Flannery O'Connor noted the same tendency in American Protestantism. In her essay entitled "Novelist and Believer," she wrote: "When Emerson decided, in 1832, that he could no longer celebrate the Lord's Supper unless the bread and wine were removed, an important step in the vaporization of religion in America was taken, and the spirit of that step has continued apace."[4] Her point is that one can only think that God is a rainbow if the word of God is torn away from the flesh it has assumed and becomes "vaporized" into something more pleasing to us, something like, well, a rainbow. When that happens, however, the Christian faith does not become secularized so much as it becomes "vaporized" into something resembling paganism, something where almost anything can be worshiped, even rainbows. As G. K. Chesterton knew, it is actually very difficult to believe in nothing for very long. However secular we think we may be, soon we will be worshiping not nothing, but anything. Above all, we will worship other gods whom we find "useful." In doing so, of course, we will have dispensed with the one community of faith whose story might have served to challenge the culture's definition of "usefulness." For this very reason, Jesus tells us that "salvation is from the Jews"(John 4:22). As Stanley Hauerwas notes,

> It is the Jews who rightly insist that salvation is not knowledge, not a gnosis, but fleshly. To be saved is to be engrafted into a body that reconstitutes us by making us part of a history not universally available. It is a history of a real people who God has made part of the kingdom through forgiveness and reconciliation. Only a people so bodily formed can survive the temptation to become a "knowledge."[5]

Becoming a "knowledge" rather than a people has been the great temptation for Christians in North America. By becoming a "knowledge" or an "explanation," we have often hoped to make Christianity less strange, turning faith into a human possibility, something that can be done, or better yet, something that can be made "useful." That is how faith becomes ethics and the mystery of grace another form of self-improvement. That is also the way we remain in control, never having to be embarrassed by the God who calls us not to be better "explainers" but instead to be a more hopeful people.

One of the reasons we resist such a call, however, is that to respond to it would set us against a hopeless culture that wants God only to be "useful" to it in pursuing its goals. Tom Long recounts John L'Heureux's troubling story, "The Expert on God," to illustrate just this point. The story's central figure is a doubt-filled Jesuit priest. Since the age of ten, he has doubted at various times the Trinity, Christ's presence in the Eucharist, the virginity of Mary, and Christ's divinity and humanity. Finally, however, he falls into a doubt that will not go away: He begins to doubt the love of God. He prays that this doubt will also recede as the others have, but his prayers yield no comfort. He prays for hope, but none comes, and so finally he is reduced to going about his duties, "driving on empty," teaching, praying, and saying Mass.

Then, one bright, clear day, after saying Mass at our Lady of Victories, he is driving home to the Jesuit house, marveling in his ironic and doubtful way over the absence of God in the world, when he comes across a terrible automobile accident. A young man lies dying, trapped in an overturned car. The priest is able to force open the crumpled car door and manages to cradle the nearly dying man in his arms. Taking a vial of holy oil from his pocket, the priest anoints the dying man, pronouncing, "I absolve you from all your sins. In the name of the Father and of the Son and of the Holy Ghost. Amen."

But, then, nothing happens. There is no shift in the world, no change in the dire situation, no word from heaven, not even any human rescuers. Only the silent world and the dying "boy's harsh, half-choked breathing." The priest begins to pray— recited prayers, rote prayers, prayers about Mary, prayers to the Father in heaven. He feels foolish, but what else can he do, what else can he say? Then come the final lines of the story, as the priest wonders,

"What would God do at such a moment, if there were a God? 'Well, do it,' he said aloud, and heard the fury in his voice. 'Say something.' But there was silence from heaven.

What could anyone say to this crushed, dying thing, he wondered. What would God say if he cared as much as I? . . . The priest could see death beginning across the boy's face. And still he could say nothing.

The boy turned—some dying reflex—and his head tilted in the priest's arms, trusting, like a lover. And at once the priest, faithless, unrepentant, gave up his prayers and bent to him and whispered, fierce and burning, 'I love you,' and continued until there was no breath, 'I love you, I love you, I love you.'"[6]

Long concludes that in this encounter, the priest has given up thinking about God as merely "useful," someone to come when we whistle, in favor of the God who calls us to attend to the mysterious presence that points to what all humanity shall be in the end.[7]

Thus, the priest begins to inhabit the story he has served all of his life, living out of its mystery and bearing its hope in a world full of suffering.

Yet we have been tempted to turn the faith into an "explanation," for other reasons besides accommodating the culture's notion of "usefulness." We have also been tempted in the hope of preventing conflict within the culture. The gospel does so often seem to make things difficult. One cannot read the Old Testament without encountering Israel's conflict with other nations, without witnessing her ongoing struggle to escape from the burden of being God's people. There is conflict on almost every page, and Israel is tempted again and again to trust in the power arrangements of the ancient Near East rather than in the provisions God has made. Things would have been so much easier if the God whom Israel worshiped could have been reduced to a mere "explanation." Then Sabbath observance, Temple worship, caring for the "widow and orphan," and refusing to worship other gods would not have caused nearly so much conflict. Then theTen Commandments would not have had to be nearly so specific or so full of those "thou shalt nots." Israel's life, however, because it inhabits this particular story, becomes a challenge to the surrounding culture, a challenge that risks saying to that culture that God is not known as "rainbow" but the God of Abraham, Isaac, and Jacob.

Yet such a challenge is not Israel's alone. The church has been engrafted into Israel's life. Even in our own time the church has been called upon to be clear about just such a challenge. The most powerful confessional document of the twentieth century is surely "The Barmen Declaration," a statement hammered out on the anvil of opposition to the Nazi effort to shape the gospel's message. It is a document that is rooted in conflict and illustrates as few other confessional statements do the extent to which the gospel calls the church to a countercultural witness, challenging that culture at the very root of its self-understanding. Barmen's first article claims

> Jesus Christ, as he is attested for us in Holy Scripture, is the one Word of God which we have to hear and which we have to trust and obey in life and in death. We reject the false doctrine, as

though the Church could and would have to acknowledge as a source of its proclamation, apart from and besides this one Word of God, still other events and powers, figures and truths, as God's revelation.[8]

"Who is God?" The old pastor's question goes to the heart of the matter. That is the question that divided the "German Christians" from the Confessing Church. Was God an explanation for the resurgent German culture, a justification for the Nazi ideology, or was God the One who came in the flesh of Jesus Christ and calls us to life in him? Barmen knew that the culture did not want to have to face such an issue, would have preferred, in fact, a declaration of faith that would have been less divisive, an explanation, perhaps, that would have allowed "other events and powers" to help define the answer. "God is a rainbow" would have done just fine and would, in any case, have given no offense. Such an explanation would have not been nearly so narrow as saying that Jesus Christ "is the *one* Word of God which we have to hear and which we have to trust and obey in life and in death." "God is a rainbow" may strike us as merely silly, but if it is true that "other events and powers" can explain God, then less silly explanations will not be long in coming.

But Barmen refused this path and proved itself in this instance to be a marvelously narrow document, and therefore full of gospel grace. The one thing it does not do is to offer an explanation of the German religious situation. Instead, it begins with scripture and simply rehearses the story, names the name, and calls to faith: "Jesus Christ, as he is attested for us in Holy Scripture" (i.e., Jesus Christ, the one whose life constitutes in memory and hope the community that has engrafted us into this story), "is the *one* Word of God" (i.e., is the scandalously single point where God's identity becomes enfleshed in human form), "which we have to hear and which we have to trust and obey in life and in death" (i.e., who defines us, and who calls us not to offer more and more sophisticated explanations but to something much more costly and much more joyful—to a life of trust and obedience in him).

In this sense, Barmen, far from being an object of nostalgia for a church that romantically longs to wear the martyr's crown, is instead a calm and surefooted guide to the future. In particular, the way suggested by its affirmation of the church as a mysterious sign of hope in the world is a path that offers direction for the church in North America. For we too struggle to keep our witness from being absorbed by a culture only too eager to dictate a peace that will exempt it from the claims of the gospel. As an example of countercultural faith, Barmen has much to teach us.

What a church might look like that struggles against the culture's efforts to absorb it into the culture's story is illustrated well in William Willimon's sermonic homage to Lesslie Newbigin. Willimon begins by noting that the conflict the gospel creates is not confined to the Old Testament. His text is from Acts 19 and rehearses the story of what happened when Paul preached in Ephesus. The conflict turns out to be both economic and theological. The goddess of the Ephesians was Artemis, who combined in her mythic abundance the "ultimate concerns" of the classical world. Her temple provided the mythological underpinnings of the Roman banking system, so she embodied prosperity and wealth. "With her multiple breasts, she held in her protective embrace bankers and debtors."[9] But Artemis was also the goddess of the hunt, the wild goddess, who protected the natural order. She was a mother goddess, protector of children. "In short, she was a perfect multi-breasted, many-faceted embodiment of our World Bank, The Humane Society, Planned Parenthood, the La Leche League, and a number of other worthy causes."[10]

The initial objections to Paul's preaching of the gospel are raised by Demetrius, the silversmith, who understands only too well that if what Paul is saying is true, the days of getting wealth from selling silver statues of Artemis are numbered. Like so many "enemies" of the gospel in the New Testament, Demetrius understands the gospel perfectly. He knows that the proclamation of Jesus Christ has economic implications. But he also knows that underlying those implications is a claim that threatens the culture's peace, a claim that imperils the deepest convictions of the culture about its gods: "You also see and hear that not only in Ephesus but in almost the whole of Asia this Paul has persuaded and drawn away a considerable number of people by saying that gods made with hands are not gods. And there is danger not only that this trade of ours may come into disrepute but also that the temple of the great goddess Artemis will be scorned"(Acts 19:26–27).

What has happened, of course, is that Ephesus has heard the good news. Willimon notes that the good news comes not in the form of communication, in which agreement or connecting are the primary goals, but rather in terms of witness, a testimony to the truth that has happened in our midst: "Witness does not attempt to 'speak to the world'; instead, witness testifies that the world belongs to God. That witness is bound to provoke conflict, not because it is difficult to understand, but rather because the content of its witness is a challenge to the world. Behind seemingly innocuous terms like 'business,' or 'politics,' or 'human values,' Christians suspect the principalities and powers to be at work."[11] The way this witness is made is in the form of a countercultural proclamation of the gospel:

> Rather than attempting to subsume the worship of Artemis into some allegedly all embracing and less threatening category like "pluralism"—saying that, though Artemis worship has much to commend it, we are all basically trying to praise the same God who some call Artemis and others call Jesus—Paul clearly demarcates the difference between the two competing deities. Paul is amazingly willing to have his witness rejected.[12]

That is precisely what makes us feel uncomfortable, what reveals our own enthrallment to the idols of North American paganism. So desperate are we to be approved by the culture, to keep its affairs running smoothly, that we will even sacrifice the offense of the gospel to enable our culture to preserve its own self-understanding, gladly turning the gospel itself into a harmless explanation. The church is eager to explain what the gospel "really means," when, in fact, the clear rejection of the gospel's message often indicates that its claims are understood only too well. "The world thus fails to hear the offense of the gospel, fails to enjoy the dignity of disbelief, and is led to believe that the difference between church and world is only one of semantics rather than an issue of idolatry."[13]

It is no small gift to be allowed "to enjoy the dignity of disbelief." For just so does the gospel take that person seriously and refuse to patronize her or him by dismissing such disbelief as if it did not matter or, worse, as if it were, in fact, real agreement. More importantly, by according someone the "dignity of disbelief," we testify to the work of the Holy Spirit, affirming that faith is finally a mystery and gift, not a product of our managerial schemes. It takes a miracle to believe the gospel, just as it always has, for "no one can say 'Jesus is Lord' except by the Holy Spirit" (1 Cor. 12:3). Yet this miracle continues to offend, especially when it resists becoming an "explanation."

Willimon notes that Paul does not preach abstractions such as "love" or "pluralism" or "diversity" to the Ephesians. These all-embracing virtues are just the culture's way of absorbing the gospel into its own story. Detached from the Word made flesh, these virtues lose any earthly significance they might have otherwise had and become "spiritual" things, vaporizing into a kind of universal spirituality that is as vague as it is self-centered. Thus, "Paul provokes conflict, not because he offers another helpful way for us to be happy, but rather because he dares to assert that one world is false, without basis, delusional ('gods made with hands are not gods') and that the real world is now present in Jesus."[14]

Such a claim will always be a challenge to the culture, for the culture has its own definitions of what is the "real world." That is why Willimon, among others, thinks that North America, if not the Western world, is more properly thought of as pagan today rather than secular: "Having relegated Christianity, along with other traditional religions, to that sphere of life called 'religious,' Western culture then claims a sphere called 'secular' or 'the natural world,' or 'the economy' which operates on principles which are allegedly immune from 'supernatural' causality."[15] But in doing so, our culture has hardly killed off the gods. Rather, they have come back more rampant than ever:

Luck becomes our secular American theology, a substitute for Providence. . . . Prometheus, Eros, Mars, Psyche, the list of deities appears to be exploding, as human activity is inflated to the level of the divine. . . . Affluent, Western people, having solved so many of life's problems like food, housing, and clothing, now beseech the gods, not for bread but for mutual orgasm.[16]

The great promise of secularity is the claim that it would enable us to avoid making divisive or painful decisions of faith by neutralizing the question, "Who is God?" What Paul recognized in Ephesus and what is becoming increasingly clear today in our own culture is that we are besieged by gods demanding our allegiance. "Paul," Willimon notes, "had the potentially unpleasant task of telling the Ephesians that the name of God was Trinity not Artemis,"[17] a task the church can never relinquish without losing its own soul. Yet it is a task that we find difficult today because it strikes us as negative, exclusive, even judgmental. What's the harm of a little Artemis worship, especially if it helps us celebrate the diversity of the culture? Who, after all, would want to appear narrow?

Yet here the gospel is scandalously narrow. Salvation really does come through the Jews. Jesus Christ really is "the one Word of God which we have to hear and which we have to trust and obey in life and in death."[18] It is scandalous. Of all people, the Jews! Of all people for a Jewish Savior to save, the Gentiles!

All attempts to achieve universality through a medium (the World Bank, the UN, "the free market") other than the existence of a witnessing people called church are to be rejected as arrogant efforts to evade the scandal that God invades the world by means of something so fragile as preaching, by people so fallible as Paul. God chooses to reconstitute the human family, to recreate the human race, overcoming the world's ways of gathering people (money, gender, race) through water and the word.[19]

In Jesus Christ, the narrow way becomes broader than the world's most universal ideals, just as the scandal of his gospel becomes an occasion, finally, for delight and joy. In this story from Acts 19, the idolatry that Paul finds in Ephesus does not bring from him ringing denunciations of the Ephesians' waywardness. Rather, Paul thinks that their idolatry is punishment enough and that what the gospel has to offer is not moralistic rules or judgmental smugness, but liberation. The gospel is good news for all people. It depicts a life that is better, fuller, more hopeful and generous, more faithful and free. It is for this reason that he is willing to risk something as provocative as contending with Artemis worship. He loves this people, and his love extends to telling them the truth about "Who is God?" This is the one question that cannot be neutralized and that love refuses to dismiss. Indeed, this is the one question that promises Sabbath rest from the daily grind of self-realization, the one question that offers us life as a gift.

Willimon concludes with a story that illustrates what is at stake in the gospel's encounter with North American paganism, and how faith causes us to reclaim the notion of "abundant life" from a culture that has understood that phrase only in terms of its own consuming. He tells of a visit to the Duke University campus of Millard Fuller, the founder of Habitat for Humanity, and how Fuller spoke one evening about the decision he and his wife made to sell everything they had and move to a poor neighborhood in Americus, Georgia. Out of that decision, Habitat for Humanity was born. Later that week, Willimon was asked, "How old were Fuller's children when he and his wife pulled up and moved to Americus?" The import of the question was slow to sink in, but behind it was the modern sentimentality that expresses one of the main tenets precious to the beliefs of North American pagans, namely, "It's fine for you to have some religious experience if you want, but it's not fine for you to drag your children into it with you, to ask them to sacrifice for your values." Willimon notes, "The person asking the question has a daughter on birth control pills at sixteen and a son who has been hospitalized for alcohol abuse." The point is, we "are all sacrificing our children to some god or another, asking our children to suffer for what we believe in, be it big breasted Artemis or Toyota, Disney, or Amway. The issue is not *if* we will worship, but *whom*."[20]

The question "Who is God?" matters. "But who do you say that I am?" Jesus asks his disciples. It is surely the happy task of the church to challenge the paganism of our own culture, even to risk provoking its most settled idolatries, by answering Jesus' question with our worship and our lives. There in the mysterious gift of our life together we witness to the life abundant that alone is ours in Jesus Christ.

8

The Language of Love: Confessing Christ before an Indifferent or Hostile Culture

*I*n his autobiography, C. S. Lewis speaks of the "baptized imagination," and he suggests that his own conversion was a conversion of the imagination before it was anything else. Prior to his confessing the faith, the things that he loved were not real and the things that were real he did not love. For him, confessing Jesus Christ meant the coming together of these two worlds; the things that he loved and the things that were real became one. This new reality was as ordinary, daily, and fleshly as the one he found formerly to be only tiresome, but it was now perceived to be something lovely, a gift that could be received and enjoyed because it was rooted in something deeper than itself, namely, in the reality of the Word made flesh.

We are used to hearing the language of conversion expressed in moral terms or even in terms of greater insight or wisdom, but Lewis implies that it is not until our sense of beauty, our sense of what he calls "holiness,"[1] is touched that we are enabled to discern what is real in what we call "the real world." Without the baptized imagination, we are always tempted to reduce the Christian faith to some moralistic exercise at self-improvement or perhaps as some special category of spiritual experience, both of which simply accept the culture's definition of what is real. But the baptized imagination invites us to see a vision of the world the culture has missed or denied, a vision that reveals the culture's definition of "the real world" to be itself an illusion. This vision of the world disclosed in Jesus Christ disrupts our culture even as it reveals hitherto unseen possibilities of a new way of living, of a more imaginative and hopeful way of life.

This is why memory is so crucial for the life of the church and why recalling the lives of the saints is so important to the church's hope. Saints stir our imaginations. They disrupt our lives. They help us see the illusions of what we often take so seriously (e.g., the effort to preserve our own lives), and they show us instead how to live imaginatively and therefore truthfully in the light of the cross and resurrection of Jesus Christ. There, they tell us, is where the *real* world begins. Without a Dietrich Bonhoeffer or Mother Teresa or Martin Luther King Jr., we might be tempted to forget what is real, yielding to the illusion that reality begins with "me" and the narratives of self I might find compelling. No, saints point to what is real, that is, they point beyond themselves to Jesus Christ and the reality rooted in his life, death, and resurrection. Their lives narrate that reality, reminding us of it in new and powerful ways, and reminding us also that discerning alternatives to the culture's definition of "the real world" is a gift that cannot be sustained apart from the community of faith and the story that community remembers. Just so are we ever dependent upon saints and the stories their lives tell, for just so do we discover in them alternatives we did not know we had, possibilities we had otherwise overlooked.[2]

In this chapter, I propose to look at the baptized imagination at work in the lives of three twentieth-century Christians who discerned possibilities of hope not apparent to the surrounding culture.

Last Testament

The first story is fairly simple and straightforward, and is more about a letter than anything else. It concerns a group of French Trappist monks who were kidnapped from their monastery in Algeria. On May 24, 1996, an organization of Islamic terrorists released a statement claiming to have "slit the throats" of seven of the monks, whom they had held hostage for some two months. Islamic terrorism, unfortunately, was a reality with which Algeria was then struggling and with which it continues to struggle. Knowing this, the superior of the monastery, Father Christian de Cherge, left with his family the following letter "to be opened in the event of my death":

> If it should happen one day—and it could be today—that I become a victim of terrorism which now seems ready to encompass all the foreigners living in Algeria, I would like my community, my Church, my family to remember that my life was given to God and to this country. I ask them to accept that the One Master of all life was not a stranger to this brutal departure. I ask them to pray for me. . . .
>
> My life has no more value than any other. Nor any less value. In any case, it has not the innocence of childhood. I have lived long enough to know that I share in the evil which seems, alas, to prevail in the world, even in that which would strike me blindly. I should like, when the time comes, to have a clear space which would allow me to beg forgiveness of God and of all my fellow human beings, and at the same time to forgive with all my heart the one who would strike me down.
>
> I could not desire such a death. It seems to me important to state this. I do not see, in fact, how I could rejoice if this people I love were to be accused too dearly for what will, perhaps, be called "the grace of martyrdom," to owe it to an Algerian, whoever he may be, especially if he says he is acting in fidelity to what he believes to be Islam. . . . It is too easy to give oneself a good conscience by identifying this religious way with the fundamental ideologies of the extremists. . . .
>
> My death, clearly, will appear to justify those who hastily judged me naïve or idealistic. . . . But these people must realize that my most avid curiosity will then be satisfied. This is what I shall be able to do, if God wills—immerse my gaze in that of the Father, to contemplate with him his children of Islam just as he sees them, all shining with the glory of Christ, the fruit of his Passion, filled with the Gift of his Spirit, whose secret joy will always be to establish communion and to refashion the likeness, delighting in the differences.
>
> For this life given up, totally mine and totally theirs, I thank God who seems to have wished it entirely for the sake of that joy in everything and in spite of everything. . . .

And you also, the friend of my final moment, who would not be aware of what you were doing. Yes, for you also I wish this "thank you"—and this adieu—to commend you to the God whose face I see in yours.

And may we find each other, happy "good thieves," in Paradise, if it pleases God, the Father of us both. Amen.[3]

What can we learn from such a letter? Perhaps the most dangerous temptation would be to romanticize Father de Cherge's words and profess envy of his martyrdom or make of him a kind of celebrity in death. The letter's astringently unsentimental faith helps us resist such silliness. Nevertheless, most of us are not surrounded by terrorists and no one threatens us with execution. So what can we learn from what Father de Cherge has to say?

It seems to me that we can learn at least three things. First of all, though Father de Cherge was surrounded by a hostile culture, he was able to discern even in its rival claims something of the truth and beauty and goodness of that culture, finding in it deep connections with the gospel of Jesus Christ. Moreover, he never doubted for a moment the image of God that was present in every Algerian. As a result, he could love this people without reservation or condition. He could even love their religion, honoring the deep and life-altering convictions of faith expressed in Islam. Though an emissary of the God of Jesus Christ, and therefore viewed as an enemy by the terrorists, he did not regard Algeria or even Islam itself as "the enemy." Rather, he thought of Islam as the "soul" of Algeria, a soul he had come to love.

Second, the faith that sustained Father de Cherge prepared him to die a good death. That is to say, his faith was not about what our culture calls success or self-invention or living happily ever after. The letter is a thank you note because the author clearly thinks his life has been a gift, not least of all to himself, a gift whose goodness can only be perceived as such as it is read in the light of Jesus Christ. And that means understanding his own death (as well as his life) as an offering to God, an offering that declares openly his belief in the One who offered himself on the cross for the whole world. In him, the purpose of human life—indeed, his own life—is disclosed.

This trust in God's purpose also allowed Father de Cherge great freedom—freedom to leave some things unsettled, including his own very uncertain future. That too could safely be offered to the God who, as the letter notes, "was not a stranger" to such brutal departures. But this trust also allowed Father de Cherge the freedom to grant those of another faith the dignity of their disagreement, never apologizing for the truth of the gospel but entrusting others, along with his own soul, to the God who is the author and finisher of every faith.

One does not have to be faced with hostile Islamic terrorists to see what a radical challenge this view represents to our own culture. If our lives are offerings to God, then we too are set free from what the culture calls freedom, that is, from the hell of belonging to ourselves. We are not doomed to a culture of hopelessness in which we struggle to "consume" ourselves or pretend to be the authors of our own lives. Rather, we are free to receive the gift of ourselves along with the gift of others from Christ's own hand, living lives and dying deaths that are generous, abundant, and, above all, grateful. So do we "publish" our deepest convictions and tell the truth by being engrafted into this story of Easter hope.

Finally, this letter depicts a communion that exists at the heart of reality whose presence enables us to discern and rejoice in the gift of other forms of communion that "the real world" regularly misses. Father de Cherge knew that at the heart of things is the triune God whose life encompasses not only French and Algerian but in some mysterious way, all the children of Abraham, willing always "to establish communion and to refashion the likeness, delighting in the differences." Lest one think this only a kind of universalizing sentimentality, this letter makes it clear that the business of establishing communion always involves dying, that is, discovering that communion where sinners find their real solidarity in sharing in Christ's suffering love for this world. Rather than leading him away from the Algerians, this vision of the triune God revealed in Jesus Christ enabled Father de Cherge to rejoice in this final solidarity with the "children of Islam," expressing the hope, even in death, even to his own executioner, that they may "find each other, happy, 'good thieves,'" in Paradise.

A Knock at the Door

In the winter of 1941, in a little village in the mountains of southern France, there came a knock on the door of the home of the Protestant pastor. The pastor was not there, but his wife answered the door. A woman, dressed poorly, almost in rags, was standing there asking for help. She was Jewish, she said, and her life was in danger. She had heard that there was someone in this village who might help her. Could she come in? The pastor's wife, Magda Trocme, answered, "Naturally, come in." Thus began the story of Le Chambon, a small village of some three thousand souls, most of whom were impoverished and largely forgotten French Calvinists, a remnant from centuries' past who nevertheless saved the lives of over five thousand Jewish refugees, mostly children, over the next four years.[4]

In the introduction to his book *Lest Innocent Blood Be Shed*, Philip Hallie asks how such goodness could have occurred in the midst of such darkness and evil. The Vichy government knew of the village and the efforts of its French Reformed pastor, Andre Trocme, to save Jewish children, and even passed that information on to the Germans who at one point arrested him. Yet Le Chambon was not touched by the Holocaust that swept the rest of Europe. Why? Hallie offers two answers. The first has to do with Trocme's pacifism. The villagers had been trained to be nonviolent, and so, Hallie thinks, they never posed much of a threat to the Nazi killing machine. But this provisional answer, as appealing as it might be, fails to explain why the Nazis were less brutal here than they were with thousands of other equally compliant populations. Second, he reports a conversation with a mathematician friend who looked at him for a moment and answered the question in another way, "It was," he said, "a miracle."[5]

This second answer at least attempts to reckon with the mystery of this goodness in the face of an unimaginable darkness. Yet, however one answers the question, Hallie is surely right in claiming that the source of this goodness worked itself out in the lives of families and individuals in Le Chambon, particularly in the life and leadership of Pastor Andre Trocme, whose faith in God and love for his parishioners provided a "city of refuge" for many in the time of trial.

Andre Trocme was born on Easter Sunday, 1901, in Saint-Quentin, in Picardy, not far from the town of Noyon where John Calvin had been born some four hundred years earlier. His mother was German and his father was from a long line of French Huguenot lace makers. During World War I, the Trocme family's home in Saint-Quentin was taken over by the Germans, and young Andre learned firsthand something of the hunger and deprivation of war. Toward the end of the war, when the Germans were retreating, he met a young German soldier who offered him some food. Andre refused the food because it came from the hand of the enemy. The soldier replied that he was not the enemy, that he had no gun, that he was a telegrapher and had refused to kill anyone. He asked Andre if he were a Christian and, upon receiving an affirmative reply, told him of his conviction that to follow Christ meant to leave violence behind. Trocme invited the soldier to a youth worship service, where they worshiped together and where the soldier was even invited to speak. His words made a lasting impression on the young French schoolboy: "One must refuse to shoot. Christ taught us to love our enemies. That is his good news, that we should help, not hurt each other, and anything you add to this comes from the Devil!"[6] Shortly after this encounter, the German soldier, whose name was Kindler, was himself killed. But Trocme never forgot his words.

Later Trocme studied theology at the University of Paris and at Union Theological Seminary in New York, even for a brief time tutoring two of John D. Rockefeller's sons in French. Upon his return to France, he married Magda Grilli, an Italian who had also studied in New York, and together they went to Mauberge, an industrial town in northern France, where Trocme had been called to serve as pastor of a small church of industrial laborers.

By 1934, the family had moved to Le Chambon, a poor village high up in the central plateau of southern France. There Trocme preached each Sunday at the Protestant Temple, and there his Calvinistic celebration of God's sovereign grace in all of life became a joyful and even encouraging word, embracing the entire community. "Behind a Huguenot sermon," writes Hallie, "is the history of a besieged minority trying to keep its moral and religious vitality against great adversity. The sermons of the pastor are one of the main sources of this vitality."[7] Trocme's confidence and his hope made those who had no reason to smile, smile, even laugh, even risk ventures they might not otherwise have tried. When the darkness of war again descended on all of Europe, the people of Le Chambon were a people prepared, able to say what Magda Trocme said that wintry day in 1941 to the first Jewish refugee who knocked on her door: "Naturally, come in."

Soon there were other refugee families and many small children. Trocme, along with others in the village, helped find them homes on farms and in attics. One day in the spring of 1941, Pastor Trocme journeyed to Marseilles, where he met with the leader of a Quaker resettlement group and offered to house even more children. Soon a kind of "underground railway" was established, such that by the end of the war, over five thousand men, women, and children had been saved.

Trocme himself did not escaped unscathed. He was arrested and imprisoned for months; he was under surveillance and received numerous threats on his life. Just before the war ended, one of his own children committed suicide. Something of the strain can be gathered from one of his letters that he wrote in February of 1943:

> [I]n the course of this summer we have been able to help about sixty Jewish refugees in our own house; we have hidden them, fed them, plucked them out of deportation groups, and often we have taken them to a safe country. You can imagine what struggles—with the authorities—what real dangers this means for us: threats of arrest, submitting to long interrogations . . .[8]

Yet under just such strain, Trocme believed, true fecundity (a favorite word of his) emerged. One's giving in Christ bears fruit in creating unforeseen possibilities for life. Later, after the war, he summed up his faith in the following words:

> Basic truth has been taught to us by Jesus Christ. What is it? The person of any one man is so important in the eyes of God, so cen-

tral to the whole of his creation, that the unique, perfect being, Jesus, a) sacrificed his earthly life for that one man in the street, and b) sacrificed his perfection by taking the blame for his sins in order to save that single man. Salvation has been accomplished without any regard to the moral value of the saved man.[9]

That "one man in the street" became for Trocme the place where Jesus Christ's presence on earth was brought into focus. The Christian faith, thought Trocme, always flew close to the ground, such that the closer we are drawn to Jesus Christ the clearer do we see the person who is suffering.

While in prison and, indeed, in the town of Le Chambon itself, Trocme had many conversations with communists, resistance leaders, and terrorists, some of whom were as violent as their Nazi enemies. To them, Trocme preached the same gospel of forgiveness and peace that he preached to his own parishioners. Though ridiculed for his faith, he staunchly maintained that Jesus was the center of history, a figure both more troubling and more joyful than any political ideology could stand. Those who followed this Christ, he thought, were called to a life of strenuous sacrifice, a life in which thought, prayer, and action would truly bear fruit in the love of neighbor and the forgiveness of enemies.

In September 1944, Le Chambon was liberated, and the refugees soon began leaving. Trocme threw himself into rebuilding the town's school, but soon the weariness from so many years of strain and the death of his own child took their toll, and he left the parish ministry, working for several years as the European secretary for the Fellowship of Reconciliation. He died in 1971 in Geneva. In his autobiographical notes, which came to light after his death, he wrote: "A curse on him who begins in gentleness. He shall finish in insipidity and cowardice, and shall never set foot in the great liberating current of Christianity." To the end he remained what the leadership of his own church had called him: "that dangerous, difficult Trocme."[10]

Pastor Trocme believed that true goodness was fecund, fruitful, that it illumined possibilities that evil or cynicism always overlooked. In this respect, the goodness of Le Chambon is perhaps best understood as a sign pointing beyond itself to that mysterious grace that refuses to let the dreary monotony of evil have the last word. In the introduction to his book, Philip Hallie tells the story of lecturing in Minneapolis on Le Chambon, when a woman stood up to ask if this was the same Le Chambon that was in the Department of the Haute-Loire in south-central France. Told that it was, the woman said, "Well, you have been speaking about the village that saved the lives of all three of my children." The room grew very silent. And then she said, "The Holocaust was storm, lightning, thunder, wind, rain, yes. And Le Chambon was the rainbow." Hallie concludes: "The rainbow is the sign God put up in heaven after the great Flood. The sign meant: '. . . never again shall all flesh be cut off.' . . . The rainbow reminds God and man that life is precious to God, that God offers not sentimental hope, but a promise that living will have the last word, not killing. The rainbow means realistic hope."[11]

What can we take from this story? Perhaps it is enough to remember the subversive possibilities that faith discloses and the marvelous fecundity of the gospel's goodness even in the face of massive terror and death. We must not sentimentalize Le Chambon, however. What happened there only makes the darkness of what happened elsewhere more visible and more horrendous. Still, what happened in this little town cannot be dismissed. If it is silly to say that "God is a rainbow," it is not silly to say that God is the God of the rainbow, the covenant-making God who will not turn his back on his creation. Le Chambon is a sign of that promise, and in that way does resemble the rainbow given to Noah.

But one other aspect of this story should not be passed over too quickly, that is, the convictions of faith that set the terms of Le Chambon's story. What happened there was miraculous at least in part because the pastor of that community thought that his little congregation were the heirs of a story that remembered "cities of refuge," that could sing about walls that came tumbling down, that worshiped One who "scattered the proud in the imagination of their hearts." That was where Pastor Trocme and the community of Le Chambon began. Because they began there, and not with assessments of their own weakness or the relative strength of the Nazi war machine, they were able to be more imaginative, more daring, more fruitful than a much wiser world thought possible.

Ruby

In the spring of 1961, the public schools in New Orleans, Louisiana, were ordered desegregated. Ruby Bridges was six years old at the time and was one of the black children chosen to enter the first grade at Frantz Elementary School. Robert Coles, who has written a good deal about Ruby, recalls:

> For days that turned into weeks and weeks that turned into months, this child had to brave murderously heckling mobs, there in the morning and there in the evening, hurling threats and slurs and hysterical denunciations and accusations. Federal marshals took her to school and brought her home. She attended school all by herself for a good part of a school year, owing to a total boycott by white families. Her parents, of sharecropper background, had just recently arrived in the great cosmopolitan port city—yet another poor black family of rural background trying to find a slightly better deal in an urban setting. They were unemployed, and, like Ruby, in jeopardy; mobs threatened them too.[12]

But Ruby persisted. After a while, even her teachers began to wonder how this six-year-old child could weather such adversity. What was the source of her serenity, her courage? Coles, who watched Ruby very closely, was himself uncertain, or rather he was certain that before long the strain of this exercise would break the child. But then one day, one of Ruby's teachers told him the following:

> I was standing in the classroom, looking out the window, and I saw Ruby coming down the street, with the federal marshals on both sides of her. The crowd was there, shouting as usual. A woman spat at Ruby but missed; Ruby smiled at her. A man shook his fist at her; Ruby smiled at him. Then she walked up the stairs, and she stopped and turned and smiled one more time!

You know what she told one of the marshals? She told him she prays for those people, the ones in that mob, every night before she goes to sleep![13]

Not long after that, Coles interviewed Ruby and asked her about her prayers. Ruby was cheerful and forthright with her answers. "Yes," she said, "I do pray for them." Why? "Because," she replied, "I go to church every Sunday, and we're told to pray for everyone, even the bad people, and so I do."[14] After a bit more prodding, Ruby talked about her faith, in particular her understanding of God:

They keep coming and saying the bad words, but my momma says they'll get tired after a while and then they'll stop coming. They'll stay home. The minister came to our house and he said the same thing, and not to worry, and I don't. The minister said God is watching and he won't forget, because he never does. The minister says if I forgive the people, and smile at them and pray for them, God will keep a good eye on everything and he'll be our protection. . . . I'm sure God knows what's happening. He's got a lot to worry about; but there is bad trouble here, and he can't help but notice. He may not rush to do anything, not right away. But there will come a day, like you hear in church.[15]

Ruby's understanding of God had been mediated to her through the prayers of her parents and the life of the worshiping community. Her help, she conceded, "came from the Lord who made heaven and earth." The courage to stand up against centuries of racial prejudice and institutionalized hatred was rooted in a story much older than the segregated South that Ruby had taken on; it was rooted in a story of children of Israel who dared to stand up against Pharaoh, of children in the fiery furnace who refused to bow down to idols, and most of all in the child whose birth in a manger unsettled the powerful of his day. In his freedom, Ruby knew herself to be free.

"All communities need heroes," write Stanley Hauerwas and Philip Kenneson, "but the church's heroes are made possible by a vision not of their own making. That is why saints are only possible in a community possessed by a story more determinative than the saints themselves."[16] The story that shaped Ruby's life was a story about a man who went to the cross, "to hang on it." Through him and the forgiving grace mediated through that cross and the community it made possible, true freedom comes. That was the story Ruby helped New Orleans remember in the spring of 1961, the story whose grace continues to disturb us today.

What does one make of Ruby's story? Again, nothing would be easier than to turn this saint into a celebrity, to think of her as a "brave, little freedom fighter" tilting against a corrupt social and political system, all the while conveniently forgetting her faith. In many ways, that is what has happened even to a person as central to American history as Martin Luther King Jr., who is known by many as a great civil rights leader (which he was) but not as a great man of faith, a pastor who called both white and black people to live out the meaning of the gospel. Ruby's life was shaped by her faith and particularly by the African-American church that supported and loved her. There she learned of this God who kept his promises and protected his children. Her pastor called upon her and prayed with her. As courageous as she was—and her courage cannot be overstated—she, nevertheless, did not walk alone, but in the company of saints who held her up in their prayers. It was the terms of the story they told her that made possible the terms of the story she lived out.

Conclusion

As Christians we confess that our story is rooted in Jesus Christ. For us, the church's imagination cannot simply be some virtue that especially creative people possess but must become instead the faithful practice by which the community points to those innovations and new possibilities that faith in God renders visible.[17] The letter of Father de Cherge, the story of Le Chambon, and the example of Ruby Bridges are all just such innovative pointers, reminding the church not only of our deepest convictions but also displaying the new alternatives for life made visible in the light of Jesus Christ. In each instance a reading was made of "basic reality" that affirmed the terms of the story as Christ-shaped. Out of those Christ-shaped terms, whether in the Algerian desert or the mountains of France or the humidity of New Orleans, fruitful and hitherto unimagined discoveries were made that revealed fruitful possibilities for life in the midst of and even in the face of death.

Moreover, in each of these stories, the terms that were laid down by the gospel were deeply subversive of the surrounding culture's understanding of what is "the real world." Yet in every instance, the world narrated in the terms of cross and resurrection contains space for possibilities "the real world" could not and did not allow for, even exposing the captivity of "the real world" to its own illusions.

In addition, in each of these stories, the courage that enabled Christian witness to be offered was sustained by the memory and hope of the church. These are stories of the Holy Spirit at work in the life of the church, not celebrities who are remembered fondly for their remarkable attributes. The community gathered by that Spirit in the name of Jesus Christ was the garden in which these flowers came to bloom.

Finally, these stories are of people whose faith flew close to the ground. In one sense they had no choice; their lives were caught up in crises of various sorts. The faith that sustained a Father de Cherge or Pastor Trocme or Ruby Bridges worked itself out in the midst of terrorism, extermination, and hatred. On the other hand, their faith was marvelously resistant to the temptation to discover some "spirituality of self." They knew the terms of the story they were living, and those terms were set in the cross of Jesus Christ. But just so did unforeseen possibilities emerge for the human community at the foot of that cross, possibilities for a new community, for a life together, for a healing of the nations.

9

The Hope That Is within Us

*I*n 1910, the United Presbyterian Church of North America attempted to describe its purpose in terms of what is called The Great Ends of the Church. The fourth of these Great Ends is "the preservation of the truth." When we hear that phrase, it almost sounds as if the church were a museum and "the truth" were some ancient artifact for which we had custodial responsibilities. But the church's interest in the truth is not merely antiquarian or pedantic anymore than it is argumentative or belligerent. The "preservation of the truth" is a form of bearing witness to the truth of Jesus Christ, a way of saying that reality is not a malleable thing we construct or something that the powers that be at any given time can devise or abolish, but is something that is rooted beyond us in the life, death, and resurrection of Jesus Christ. To tell the truth, we believe, is finally to come to terms with his life, or, as the gospel puts its so eloquently, to follow him. It is to enter upon a definite way, a way that is not neutral or vague but that brings us face to face with the intrusive claims of his life on our own. Those claims imperiously insist, for example, that Jesus' love for his enemies is true, not just nice or heroically impressive but true in that such love reveals the very character of God's own life. To be sure, we do not "preserve" that truth. The church cannot do that. If anything, such truth sustains the church. But to bear such a witness is to understand something of what is at stake in the church's interest in the truth. If we no longer can confess this truth of Jesus Christ or think it only a matter of indifference, then, as Ivan Karamazov would only be too happy to remind us, anything can be true. The truth will become whatever I am able to enforce.

So where does that leave us with the old pickup truck and its bumper sticker? "God said it, I believe it, and that settles it!" In a way, this book has sought to propose an alternative to that bumper sticker's summation of the gospel's account of the truth. Admittedly, the alternative is not nearly so glib. Indeed, what this book has proposed is curiously resistant to any summation of the gospel that would allow us to bring a conversation to a close before Jesus himself does. Such glibness, which our culture takes as a sign of certainty, often obscures rather than illumines the messiness of God's incarnate truth. Moreover, such glibness can all too easily encourage us to dismiss others as if we ourselves were exempt from the claims of this truth. Not surprisingly, it is the glib certainty of both Pharisee and disciple that Jesus regularly frustrates with on his determined journey to the cross. There he complicates our lives enormously by his decision to live out the truth of God's love for sinners. There is where he tells the truth we find so messy, so inconveniently incarnate. Indeed, there in that community of the Crucified is where the integrity of our "enemies" is most fully guaranteed. And there Jesus does not offer us a dismissive slogan. Rather, he draws us into his own life.

This means that the answer to the bumper sticker is not another slogan, not even an invitation to "niceness" or "tolerance" or "openness." Rather, this answer must imaginatively engage the world of that bumper sticker with the hope of the gospel, a hope that has made a new kind of community possible. That is why the first task of the church in a world addicted to slogans is to be, simply, the church. Having been drawn into the life of Jesus Christ, our first task is not to become socially useful or to seek some other way of justifying ourselves before the world. Indeed, the judgment on such efforts is terrible, for they soon render the church as boring and hopeless in its own life as the surrounding culture. Just so does salt lose its savor. No, Jesus' word is truth. In exhibiting the truth of our life in him before the world, we bear witness to the miraculous life together that is made possible by the risen Lord who has overcome the principalities and powers that otherwise would seek to rule our lives. Far from being a withdrawal from the

world and the issues that confront us, the church's witness to this
Lord through its own life engages the principalities and powers
most deeply. Why would such principalities and powers ever fear
a church that sought only to trade in slogans or exhort others to a
superior righteousness? Or why should our culture even bother
with a church that finds the whole business of the truth too difficult, a church that is willing to settle for a neutrality that risks no
claims and makes no judgments? Would Dietrich Bonhoeffer have
been put to death or even found subversive if he had not confessed
with the church that "Jesus Christ, as he is attested for us in Holy
Scripture, is the one Word of God which we have to hear and
which we have to trust and obey in life and in death"?[1] Would
Ruby Bridges have represented such a threat to the surrounding
culture if she had not believed what she was taught in Sunday
school? Is it not precisely when the church lives out the truth of
the gospel in its own life that it engages the world's attention most
daringly?

But when has it ever done that? And when it has tried to do that,
hasn't the church become imperialistic itself, intolerant of other
claims and protective of its own interests? Wouldn't the church and
the world be better off if the church became more modest in the
matter of the truth and contented itself with a certain usefulness to
the culture in works of compassion and mercy?

The first congregation I ever served was located near a state
school for the mentally retarded. At one point in my ministry there,
the congregation was approached by the school to take on one or
two young men as our "friends." These men were retarded, in one
case mildly and in the other case more severely. We were to
"socialize" them, to help them learn appropriate behavior in a public setting. The church was thought to be ideal for this, I suspect,
because it was deemed a safe place.

One of the men who came into our church's life was named
Cecil. Cecil was severely retarded and his face was profoundly dis-
figured. An elderly couple would pick him up on Sunday morning
and make sure he was dressed in his Sunday best and bring him to
church. There they would sit next to him and shepherd him through
the service. There was nothing dangerous about this. Cecil was our
project and we were helping him out. Or so we thought.

For the most part, Cecil liked church. He would smile in a lopsided sort of way during his favorite hymns. He liked dressing up in his suit, and though he could not read or write, he had no trouble making it through worship. And in truth, we came to like Cecil. He was sort of our mascot, we thought—a friendly face who symbolized our goodwill.

A couple of Sundays passed before I heard that Cecil was ill. He had been diagnosed with a virulent form of cancer that required the immediate amputation of his arm. He was in the state hospital in Galveston, and it was there I went as his pastor to visit him. It was raining that day, and I remember thinking as I drove that this was a fool's errand. Something had changed. Cecil the project had somehow become Cecil the person. When I entered his hospital room, there was a single bed, a couple of lockers, a tile floor, and Cecil. He smiled at me when I came in, his dumb, lopsided smile. We talked for a while and I asked him if he was afraid. He nodded his head yes, and began to weep. I held him as his shoulders heaved. What had happened? It had all seemed so nice and safe. Cecil was our project and we were just playing church, but now this project had become a life, a life that had a claim on our hearts, a life that had become a gift to us. I had no words. When Cecil was a project, I was full of words. But now I was empty. He had become a mysterious gift and I did not know what to say.

"I want to go home," Cecil told me. I sat with him in the silence for a moment before asking, "Well, where's your suit, Cecil?" He got off the bed and opened one of the lockers and showed me his neatly pressed brown suit. He stood before it as if it were some trophy he had won. He came back to the bed and put his head on the pillow and was quiet. "Cecil," I said, "you can't come home until you have a tie to go with your suit. You need a tie. I took my tie off and folded it on the pillow beside his head. "Here, Cecil; it's a gift. You will wear it and you will come home." I prayed with him that afternoon as the shadows lengthened and the evening came. I prayed with him no longer as a volunteer or even as a friend. I prayed with him as his pastor. And in my prayer I found myself speaking the language of Good Friday and Easter, the language of death and resurrection.

Not long after that Cecil died. His memorial service was at the church, and it was packed with folk whom he had touched. He was buried in his suit and tie. We thought we were doing such a good deed, such an easy thing, an act of compassion that really cost us very little. But Cecil taught us differently. He taught us that the church lives as it bears witness to the truth of Jesus' death and resurrection, that that truth enables us to love one another in all our difference and strangeness, not out of some "goodwill" or risk-free compassion. Cecil helped us see the miracle and the mystery of being Christ's church, something we had almost forgotten in our eagerness to be of service. Cecil enlarged our Christian imagination.

This book began with a quotation from Eberhard Arnold, the founder of the Bruderhof community: "Truth without love kills, but love without truth lies."[2] Arnold's point is not that truth needs to be gentle and kind or that love needs to have a stronger backbone, but that truth and love are rooted in the story of Jesus Christ. In him, there is simply no risk-free way of telling or living the truth.

The same gospel story, however, also tells us that it is impossible to love unless that love takes on the cross-shaped truth that Jesus Christ reveals in his own body and blood. Otherwise, even our deepest loves become something less than miraculous, something less costly, a way of telling a lie to ourselves. That is why the gospel, which speaks so much about love, is so entirely unsentimental. The love it speaks of is revealed in the cross. That is why the opposite of the gospel always ends in sentimentality. It is the way we learn to lie to ourselves, the way we try to convince ourselves that love has no risks or costs. As pornography is to art, Flannery O'Connor would remind us, so is sentimentality to faith.[3]

Cecil's life and death were quite unsentimental. The truth he enabled us to see was full of Christ's love for sinners, and the love he bore to us was utterly truthful in its cruciform shape. Cecil enlarged our imagination in the same way that saints have always done that work, namely, by helping us to see Jesus, a dangerous figure who often lurks in places in which we think he has no business being. That is why seeing Jesus has always been such a humbling business, even as it has been so full of surprising hope. It may indeed sound prideful to say one has learned humility, but humility is ever the gift of him who displaces us from the center of our world. That is what sets humility apart from a pious or pretended modesty. True humility is a way of seeing, even a way of hoping. A pluralism of self-imposed modesty can be a despairing thing, pretending as it does that our deepest differences do not matter. Disagreements can only be debated civilly, we tell ourselves, if the whole matter of truth is left outside the door. But that humility, which is the gift of the cross, is a strangely confident and liberating gift. The cross sets us free to engage our very real differences with others in the knowledge that even our "enemies" have been reconciled to Jesus Christ by his death and that whatever our differences, the line that separates "us" from "them" cannot be taken with complete seriousness. We are his. We are his not because we say we are his, but because he has claimed this world as his own. We are free then to engage the other about what matters the most—the truth—knowing that his truth is not an argument to be won or a debate to be settled but a way of loving his world.

Such a conversation is the way the church preserves the truth. Indeed, it is the way we hope. Easter is not just a pleasant story we have contrived to believe. It is, rather, the truth about this world and God's love for it. The old Calvinists were right about that. We are predestined to be loved by God. That is our inescapable fate. The world may be as embarrassed to learn of this good news as the church is to tell it. We all would prefer a more modest and comfortable nihilism that acquiesced in our own triviality and left us with the illusion that we were still in control. Preserving the truth, however, is the way the church witnesses to the scandal of the gospel, the way the church remembers God's intrusive grace in Jesus Christ. But it is also the way the church insists on the dignity of human life, the gift and calling of being human. Even that gift is not something we can give ourselves but comes to us only through the mysterious grace of our Lord Jesus Christ. To miss that gift is to miss the gospel itself, something that would seem to be impossible, but something that our modest neutrality, our pluralisms of despair, our grim moral exhortations enable us to do every day. But God, thank God, is sneaky. He keeps sending us Cecils, over whom we stumble and fall, and so, from our knees, gain a better perspective.

Notes

1. Confessing Christ as an Act of Love

1. Lesslie Newbigin, *Truth to Tell: The Gospel as Public Truth* (Grand Rapids: Wm. B. Eerdmans Publishing Co., 1991), 25.
2. Harold Bloom, *The American Religion: The Emergence of the Post-Christian Nation* (New York: Simon & Schuster, 1992), 37.
3. Emily Dickinson, "Those—dying then" (no. 1551).
4. Shakespeare, *Macbeth,* act 1, scene 3.
5. A formulation attributed to Richard Rorty.
6. The Heidelberg Catechism, *The Constitution of the Presbyterian Church (U.S.A.),* Part I: *Book of Confessions* (Louisville, Ky.: Office of the General Assembly, Presbyterian Church (U.S.A.), 1999), 4.001.
7. Fyodor Dostoyevsky, *The Brothers Karamazov,* trans. Constance Garnett (New York: Signet, 1980), 219, 226.
8. Ibid., 332.
9. Ibid., 333.

2. Loving Our Enemies

1. Jean Bethke Elshtain, "The Bright Line: Liberalism and Religion," *New Criterion* March 1999, 4.
2. Cited in Stanley Hauerwas, *After Christendom? How the Church Is to Behave if Freedom, Justice, and a Christian Nation Are Bad Ideas* (Nashville: Abingdon Press, 1991), 30.
3. Cited in Elshtain, "Bright Line," 12.
4. Elshtain, "Bright Line," 11.
5. Newbigin, *Truth to Tell,* 56.
6. Ralph Wood, "Hearing the Voice of God" (convocation sermon at Samford University, 23 September 1997).
7. Ibid.
8. Ibid.

3. The Arrogance of Modesty and the End of Autonomy

1. Cited in William Willimon, "Formed by Saints," *Christian Century*, 7–14 February 1996, 136.
2. Willimon, "Formed by Saints," 136.
3. Ibid., 137.
4. "A living tradition then is an historically extended, socially embodied argument." Alasdair MacIntyre, *After Virtue: A Study in Moral Theory* (Notre Dame, Ind.: University of Notre Dame Press, 1984), 222.
5. Willimon, "Formed by Saints," 136.
6. Ibid., 137.
7. Ibid.
8. Lesslie Newbigin, *The Gospel in a Pluralist Society* (Grand Rapids: Wm. B. Eerdmans Publishing Co., 1989), 82.
9. Ibid., 83.
10. The classic formulation is from G. E. Lessing: "Accidental truths of history can never become the proof of necessary truths of reason."
11. Cited in James B. Torrance, *Worship, Commmunity, and the Triune God of Grace* (Downers Grove, Ill.: InterVarsity Press, 1996), 76.
12. Dietrich Bonhoeffer, *Life Together* (San Francisco: Harper & Row, 1954), 114.
13. Eugene Peterson, "Eat This Book: The Holy Community at Table with the Holy Scripture," *Theology Today* 56, no. 1 (April 1999): 7.
14. Flannery O'Connor, "The River," in *The Complete Stories* (New York: Farrar, Straus & Giroux, 1987), 168.

4. Trinitarian Life

1. Fred Craddock, "What We Do Not Know," *Journal for Preachers*, Advent 1998, 33.
2. Ibid., 35.
3. Torrance, *Worship, Community, and the Triune God*, 39.
4. Craddock, "What We Do Not Know," 35–36.
5. Colin E. Gunton, *The One, the Three, and the Many: God, Creation, and the Culture of Modernity* (New York: Cambridge University Press, 1993), 101.
6. The term is Friedrich Nietzsche's and represents what is in his view the most basic human motivation.
7. Allan Bloom, *Closing of the American Mind: How Higher Education Has Failed Democracy and Impoverished the Souls of Today's Students* (New York: Simon & Schuster, 1987), 38–39.
8. Gunton, *One, the Three, and the Many*.

5. Telling the Truth as an Act of Faith

1. Lesslie Newbigin, *Foolishness to the Greeks: The Gospel and Western Culture* (Grand Rapids: Wm. B. Eerdmans Publishing Co., 1986), 89.
2. Ibid., 90.
3. Peter Singer, *Rethinking Life and Death: The Collapse of Our Traditional Ethics* (New York: St. Martin's Press, 1994), 220.
4. Ibid.
5. Newbigin, *Gospel in a Pluralist Society,* 15.
6. Newbigin, *Foolishness to the Greeks,* 30.
7. Newbigin, *Gospel in a Pluralist Society,* 17.
8. MacIntyre, *After Virtue.*
9. Newbigin, *Truth to Tell,* 27.
10. Newbigin, *Gospel in a Pluralist Society,* 49.
11. Ibid., 48.
12. Ibid., 77.
13. Ibid., 126.
14. Ibid., 22.
15. Ibid., 127.

6. Other Voices, Other Claims

1. Terry Muck, *Alien Gods on American Turf* (Wheaton, Ill.: Victor Books, 1990).
2. The terms "descriptive pluralism" and "prescriptive pluralism" come from Alister McGrath, *A Passion for Truth: The Intellectual Coherence of Evangelicalism* (Downers Grove, Ill.: InterVarsity Press, 1996), 204.
3. Newbigin, *Gospel in a Pluralist Society,* 9–10.
4. McGrath, *Passion for Truth,* 214.
5. Ibid., 216–17.
6. John Budziszewski, *True Tolerance* (New Brunswick, N.J.: Transaction Publishers, 1992), 7.
7. Ibid.
8. Newbigin, *Gospel in a Pluralist Society,* 181.
9. Ibid., 159.

7. Feeling Uncomfortable at Home

1. Bloom, *American Religion,* 37.
2. Ibid., 49.
3. Cf. Stanley Hauerwas, "The Democratic Policing of Christianity," *Pro Ecclesia* 3 (Spring 1994): 216.

4. Flannery O'Connor, "Novelist and Believer," in *Mystery and Manners* (New York: Noonday Press, 1969), 161.
5. Haverwas, "The Democratic Policing of Christianity," 231.
6. Thomas G. Long, "When Half Spent Was the Night: Preaching Hope in the New Millennium," in *Journal for Preachers* (Easter 1999), 19. Used by permission of the author. Quotation from John L'Heureux taken from "The Expert on God," in *Comedians,* by John L'Heureux (Penguin, 1990).
7. Ibid.
8. "Theological Declaration of Barmen," *Book of Confessions,* 8.11–12.
9. William Willimon, "Preaching as Missionary Encounter with North American Paganism," in *Journal for Preachers* (Easter 1999): 3.
10. Ibid.
11. Ibid., 5.
12. Ibid.
13. Ibid.
14. Ibid., 6.
15. Ibid., 7.
16. Ibid.
17. Ibid., 6.
18. *Book of Confessions,* 8.11.
19. Willimon, "Preaching as Missionary Encounter," 8.
20. Ibid., 9.

8. The Language of Love

1. C. S. Lewis, *Surprised by Joy: The Shape of My Early Life* (New York: Harcourt Brace Jovanovich), 179.
2. Cf. Stanley Hauerwas and Philip Kenneson, "Jesus and/as the Nonviolent Imagination of the Church," *Pro Ecclesia* 1, no. 1 (Fall 1992): 76–88.
3. Father Christian de Cherge, "Last Testament," *First Things,* August/ September 1996, 21.
4. Philip Paul Hallie, *Lest Innocent Blood Be Shed: The Story of the Village of Le Chambon and How Goodness Happened There* (New York: HarperPerennial, 1994), xiii, 120.
5. Ibid., xxi.
6. Ibid., 61.
7. Ibid., 172.
8. Ibid., 147.
9. Ibid., 160.
10. Ibid., 266.
11. Ibid., xvii.
12. Robert Coles, *The Moral Life of Children* (Boston: Atlantic Monthly Press, 1986), 22.

13. Ibid., 22–23.
14. Ibid., 23.
15. Ibid., 24.
16. Hauerwas and Kenneson, "Jesus and/as the Non-violent Imagination," 82.
17. Ibid., 81.

9. The Hope That Is within Us

1. *Book of Confessions,* 8.11.
2. Cited in Johann Christoph Arnold, *Seventy Times Seven: The Power of Forgiveness* (Farmington, Pa.: Plough Publishing House, 1997), 145.
3. Flannery O'Connor, "The Church and the Fiction Writer," in *Mystery and Manners,* 148.